CW00539875

'*Late Spring*, directed and co-written by Yasujiro Ozu, was released in 1949, which makes it an old film, or a film that has been new for a long time . . .' In this startling new book Adam Mars-Jones dives into the mysteries of a single classic Japanese film and comes back with any number of surprises. Sometimes (he says) works of art need to be defended against their advocates, and great films rescued from their reputations. Masterpieces are not fragile but robust. They can stand up to more than a reverent dusting.

Adam Mars-Jones writes fiction and non-fiction, and reviewed films for the *Independent* between 1986 and 1997. *Noriko Smiling* follows closely on the heels of *Cedilla*, the second novel in the *Pilcrow* sequence, making 2011 an *annus productibilis* if not necessarily *mirabilis* for him. This wayward talent has moved from a snail-like work-rate to a gallop, and should slow down before he overtakes Trollope or breaks a leg.

Adam Mars-Jones

—

# NORIKO SMILING

Notting Hill Editions

Published in 2011
by Notting Hill Editions Ltd
Newcombe House, 45 Notting Hill Gate
London W11 3LQ

Designed by FLOK Design, Berlin, Germany
Typeset by CB editions, London

Printed and bound
by Memminger MedienCentrum, Memmingen, Germany

A CIP record for this book
is available from the British Library
ISBN 978-1-907-90345-8

www.nottinghilleditions.com

# — NORIKO SMILING —

*or*, It's the quiet ones you have to watch

*L* *ate Spring*, directed and co-written by Yasujiro Ozu, was released in 1949, which makes it an old film, or a film that has been new for a long time.

I first saw it in 2010, when it was already past its sixtieth birthday. I'd seen a couple of other Ozu films before it, perhaps a dozen Kurosawas, some in cinemas on first release, and a small handful of Mizoguchis. I saw a few contemporary releases, such as *Tampopo*, as a working critic, but I can hardly be accused of being an expert on Japanese film. A box set of Naruse waits serenely by the DVD player, its shrink-wrap reflecting the light without any crinkle of reproach.

So what are the odds of finding new things to talk about in so elderly a product, staple of so many film-studies curricula? Pretty much a hundred per cent, I'd say. I'm quietly confident. This is partly because of the nature of the film itself, glancing, wayward, and partly because of the way Westerners look at art works from Eastern cultures, rather passively assuming their mysteriousness.

In the 1980s there was an act on the London music circuit called the Frank Chickens, two Japanese women who had quite a little following, in

Hackney, in Camden, for their performances of quirky songs (*We are ninja, not geishas / That's not what you expect*). When they came on stage they would acknowledge the previous performers, bowing demurely and saying, 'Thank you for authentic display of traditional folk culture.'

Perhaps Edward Said slipped the Frank Chickens a tenner to insert this neat little mirroring of Orientalist attitudes into their act.

In general, even so, I have doubts about the usefulness of Said's term 'orientalism', as expounded with particular reference to the Middle East in his 1978 book of that name. It reduces all the ways in which cultures can misunderstand each other to mechanisms of control, when history shows us something closer to a hall of mirrors than a shooting gallery. There are so many ways of getting the wrong end of the stick, and relatively few of them go on to involve beating someone over the head with it.

Japanese cinema arrived as an international phenomenon when *Rashomon* won a major European prize in 1951, though David Desser's analogy seems to run away with him when he describes the importance of the moment: 'Admiral Perry and his Black Ships steamed into Tokyo Bay in 1853 and forced the opening of Japan to the West. Akira Kurosawa's *Rashomon* came steaming into the Venice Film Festival and opened up the West to Japanese films.' It's true that there were no shots fired on either occasion, but at least Perry was in a position to make threats.

From this distance it's not hard to see that one of the reasons for Kurosawa's impact was that he himself had been so much influenced by American films. His reputation hasn't declined in any dramatic way, but two rather quieter directors, Mizoguchi and Ozu, have come to be seen as part of a more profoundly Japanese tradition.

According to Donald Richie (in his 1959 book *The Japanese Film*, co-written with Joseph L. Anderson), the perception of Ozu as uniquely Japanese worked against his becoming known internationally. It was felt that the West couldn't possibly appreciate anything so 'truly Japanese', but also that trying to get Ozu's excellence recognised, and then failing, would be actively disgraceful. Better not to make the attempt.

Conversely, in 1954, when Kinugasa's *Gate of Hell* won the Grand Prize at Cannes, the domestic press felt mortified rather than triumphant. The film had made no one's 'Ten Best' lists of 1953, so wasn't this foreign accolade in fact an insult, barely disguised? Outsiders seemed to be saying that Japanese critics didn't know their business.

Ozu's *Tokyo Story* (1953) is regularly named one of the best films ever made, but there are plenty of people who, like me, prefer *Late Spring* (*Banshun*) from 1949. The elements that make up Ozu's late style are fully present. So long after its first release *Late Spring* is still limber and elusive. Being in black-and-white can have a paradoxical effect on the feel of an old film, making it seem undated in other ways because so obviously dated in one, rather as Andy Warhol's white fright wig gave him a spectral look of youth.

What happens on screen isn't the same thing as what happens to the spectators of a film while they watch it, but the question is worth asking: what is it that happens in the film? This is the synopsis given in *The Japanese Film*:

A college professor lives in Kamakura with his twenty-seven-year-old daughter. His wife having recently died, he now begins to think that it is time for his daughter to marry, before she is too old. At last she agrees and they find her a husband. Before her wedding they take a trip to Kyoto, as if to sever old relationships before her new life begins. Then, after she marries, he returns to his now-empty house and his new life alone. This film marked the emergence of Ozu's new postwar style. There was a virtual elimination of plot in the interests of creating character and atmosphere. Yet, with almost no story in the usual sense of the word, the film's development is quite complex.

It becomes easier to emphasise plotlessness if you've whittled plot down yourself, to a barely surviving nub. Most people who have seen the film will flesh out the skeletal family by remembering the heroine's aunt, probably with irritation, since she's the one who puts

the idea of her marriage firmly on the agenda, turning it from a freely floated possibility into something
which must be dealt with one way or the other.

There are probems even with so compressed an
account. Where is the evidence for the death of the
professor's wife being a recent event? I can't find it,
however many times I see the film. Perhaps there are
visual indications of mourning detectable to a long-
time resident of Japan, but the few faint references
to the dead woman make her seem distant in time, if
only because they are so faint and few.

Donald Richie has spent most of his life in Japan, and started reviewing films for the *Japan Times*
in the 1950s. His has been a dominant voice in the
interpretation of Japanese films, and Japanese culture generally, but he's a rather inconsistent critic,
sometimes seeing the films very clearly, sometimes
(particularly in the case of Ozu) treating them as
mystical objects.

That meddling aunt emerges prominently from
Roger Ebert's plot summary:

Shukichi [Somiya] is a professor, a widower, absorbed in his
work. His unmarried daughter, Noriko, runs his household
for him. Both are perfectly content with this arrangement until
the old man's sister declares that her niece should get married.
Noriko is, after all, in her mid-20s; in Japan in 1949, a single
woman that old is approaching the end of her shelf life. His sister warns the professor that after his death Noriko will be left
alone in the world; it is his duty to push her out of the nest and

find a husband who can support her. The professor reluctantly agrees. When his daughter opposes any idea of marriage, he tells her he is also going to remarry. That is a lie, but he will sacrifice his own comfort for his daughter's future. She marries.

And that, essentially, is what happens on the surface in Yasujiro Ozu's *Late Spring* (1949). What happens at deeper levels is angry, passionate and – wrong, we feel, because the father and the daughter are forced to do something neither one of them wants to do, and the result will be resentment and unhappiness. Only the aunt will emerge satisfied . . .

This is rather a partisan account. Nothing in the film spells out with any clarity that the future will be miserable both for the bride in her new home and for the father left alone. Most viewers, admittedly, get a sense of pathos, even bleakness, from their last sight of the father, using a knife on an apple, whose scroll of peel he seems to want to keep intact until the moment that it falls to the floor. The final shot of the film shows the sea, transcending human suffering or indifferent to it, either absorptive or rebuking of our small concerns.

There's a famous statement in the Richie and Anderson book about the director's concentration on domestic issues: 'In every Ozu film the whole world exists in one family. The ends of the earth are no more distant than [the] outside of the house.' *Late Spring* disproves this in any fuller synopsis, with Noriko's lively, unthreatened friendship with Aya, a divorcée.

Western critics have gradually woken up to the fact that Ozu breaks as many rules as he keeps, and that he makes up plenty of his own. Being Japanese is not a state with a single dimension.

Cultural skewings of reputation happen all the time. In fact the sane-seeming episodes of cultural transmission (the Beatles conquer America) are outnumbered by the other kind: Jerry Lewis storming Paris, Norman Wisdom marching through Albania.

How sensible would Japanese critics seem on the subject of Ivy Compton-Burnett, for instance, if her novels happened to have a wild vogue in Japan? If they kept saying how English she was, we would be hard put to deny it. But those books would be a very eccentric source of ideas about family life and domestic conversation.

Japanese cinema, as we have come to understand it from that post-war golden age, and despite Kurosawa's strong counter-example, is hushed, serene and inexplicit. It takes a particular interest in women, their lives and choices.

Ozu first directed a film in 1927, and by the time of the late style inaugurated by *Late Spring* had more or less dispensed with camera movement. Angles are invariably low, at eye level if your eye happens to be a couple of feet above a *tatami* mat. Periodically there will be a cut to a view of a room or a courtyard, a shot humming with neutrality which nevertheless bears some relationship to the reaction shot, except for the fact that what we see does not react. A reaction shot speeds up the assimilation of action, by telling us what we should be feeling – these shots slow the narrative down, with their mute appeals to the inanimate.

The most famous shot of this sort, and one of the most famous moments in *Late Spring*, comes when the heroine Noriko seems finally to accept that she must leave her father. She lies awake in the room she is sharing with him in an inn in Kyoto. The camera gives us two shots of a vase, holding each shot for quite a few seconds.

Paul Schrader, who started out as a critic before becoming a screenwriter (*Taxi Driver*) and director (*Mishima*), makes rather a meal of this shot.

The vase is stasis, a form which can accept deep, contradictory emotion and transform it into an expression of something unified, permanent, transcendent. The decisive action – the miracle of the tears – has little meaning in itself but serves to prove the strength of the form. The transcendental style, like the vase, is a form which expresses something deeper than itself, the inner unity of all things.

Because similar elements appear in Ozu's films in different combinations, it can be tempting to treat him as sort of *ikebana* formalist – exploring the emotional pay-off that follows from the placement of a single chrysanthemum just so. Schrader takes this idea even further into abstraction, so that any emotional impact gets lost in the inner unity of all things, and Noriko's miraculous tears (why miraculous?) lose all possible moisture content.

Ozu has the reputation of having calculated his effects meticulously in advance, but the original script for *Late Spring* doesn't actually feature the vase. So perhaps the release of Noriko's feelings meant more to the director than it does to Schrader.

Richie's reading of the vase shot is remarkably similar to Schrader's:

The image of the vase in the darkened room to which Ozu returns at the end of *Late Spring* serves not only to bridge the transition between Setsuko Hara equitable and Setsuko Hara near tears, but also to contain and to an extent create our own emotions. Empathy is not the key here. To be sure we do imaginatively project our own consciousness onto another being, but this is perhaps a secondary effect. Primary to the experience is that in these scenes empty of all but *mu*, we suddenly apprehend what the film has been about, i.e. we suddenly apprehend life. This happens because such scenes occur when at least one important pattern in the picture has become clear. In *Late Spring* the daughter has seen what will happen to her: she will leave her father, she will marry. She comes to understand this precisely during the time that both we and she have been shown the vase. The vase itself means nothing, but its presence is also a space and into it pours our emotion.

*Mu* is a Zen term meaning nothingness. It's written on Ozu's gravestone, and the '*mu* shot' seems to be one of the approved terms for his trademark way of cutting to objects or pieces of decor.

Take away the devotional incense, and most of this is amazingly weak. We suddenly 'apprehend life' in certain scenes of vistas or objects 'because' such scenes occur when at least one important pattern in the picture has become clear. This is a description which could apply to most scenes in most films. The explanatory force of that 'because' is so weak that it belongs in the warehouse next to the chocolate fireguard.

Richie's book on Ozu came out after Schrader's essay on 'Transcendental Style' in the work of three directors (the other two are Bresson and Dreyer), but if, as Schrader says, 'whatever we in the West know about Japanese film, and how we know it, we most likely owe to Donald Richie', then he is following Richie rather than leading him.

He's not being left behind, though. Richie never went as far as Schrader in crying up a spiritual aspect in Ozu's work. Schrader takes the Zen note struck by Richie and runs with it – in fact running doesn't do justice to his athleticism. He's airborne, he's underwater, he's in outer space. He asks, 'Do Ozu's films express the Transcendent, or do they express Ozu, Zen culture, and man's experience of the Transcendent?' Apparently there's no third possibility. It's odd to be force-fed such uncoercive ideas. Sometimes Schrader seems like a true believer who will use the thumbscrew on you if you don't accept the principle of non-attachment.

His answer to his own question goes like this: 'In Ozu's films it seems that his personality was enveloped by Zen culture, and that Zen culture was enveloped by a transcending reality, like the fish who ate the fish who ate the fish.' This isn't just Zen, it's Zen triple distilled, at industrial strength. It's a dose sufficient to stupefy the uninitiated.

Paul Schrader is from a Calvinist background and didn't see a film until he was eighteen. He had a panic attack before the showing, fearing that his immortal soul was at stake. The film was *The Absent-Minded Professor*, a Disney comedy in which Fred McMurray plays the inventor of a super-resilient compound. After that there was no going back for Schrader. Since that first exposure film has been at least as much a sacrament for him as an art form or an entertainment, though flubber is a strange stand-in for the consecrated host. Can we at least agree that he is a special case?

He hasn't been the only one ringing the temple bells, though. In the BFI's rather ramshackle booklet published in 1972, early days for the Ozu cult, Marvin Zeman says straight out that 'the criteria one must use for Ozu should be those of Japanese art and not cinematic art'. Even this formula isn't extreme enough to satisfy him, and he goes on to analyse Ozu's work in terms of four basic Zen moods.

It's another case of fish eating fish eating fish. Ozu's films are wholly enclosed by Japanese art, which is wholly enclosed by Zen aesthetics. How can we possibly approach them except on our knees, in reverent mindlessness?

The four moods are as follows. *Sabi*: quietness, solitude. *Wabi*: contemplative sadness. *Mono-no-aware*: *wabi* intensified, so perhaps meaning an epiphany of beauty which is also a revelation of loss. Then there's *yugen* to complete the set: the awareness of something you'll never know.

*Mono-no-aware* seems to be the key term in this version of Ozu's sensibility. It's a Zen state with its own Wikipedia entry. The idea ('awareness of *mujo* or the transience of things and a bittersweet sadness at their passing') is a venerable one, dating back to the eighteenth century, but Wikipedia links it firmly to Ozu and even connects it implicitly with what happens in *Late Spring*: 'The quintessentially "Japanese" director Yasujiro Ozu was well known for creating a sense of *mono no aware*, frequently climaxing with a character saying a very understated "ii tenki desu ne" (It is fine weather, isn't it?), after both a familial and societal paradigm shift, such as a daughter being married off, against the backdrop of a swiftly changing Japan.' Ozu is not just Japanese but 'Japanese', and the fish eats its own tail. *Mono-no-aware* is used to define Ozu, and Ozu is used to exemplify *mono-no-aware*.

If we were pushed as strongly towards expressions of resignation in Shakespeare as we are in Ozu

(I'm thinking of the mother's 'Life is disappointing, isn't it?' in *Tokyo Story*) then there would be neon signs in theatre foyers flashing *Ripeness Is All* before every performance of *King Lear*.

It seems more sensible to start from the notion that Ozu's films are not pieces of Zen but pieces of cinema. They may have a particular relationship with film language but they still work, or we would have no prospect of enjoying them, however strongly their transcendental virtues were touted. Even if art has its roots in the sacred, there is no possibility of turning it back into a purely religious experience, any more than you can turn cider back into apples.

David Thomson is properly secular in his approach, but even he makes out that 'our' films (by which he means American ones, now that he lives there) worship a centrifugal energy, so that Ozu's cinema with its centripetal tendencies of compromise and acceptance will always be essentially alien, despite the admiration it commands. This from the *New Biographical Dictionary of Film*:

Our stories promote the hope of escape, of beginning again, of beneficial disruptions. One can see that energy – hopeful, and often damaging, but always romantic – in films as diverse as *The Searchers*, *Citizen Kane*, *Mr. Smith Goes to Washington*, *Run of the Arrow*, *Rebel Without a Cause*, *Vertigo*, *Bonnie and Clyde*, *Greed*, and *The Fountainhead*. No matter how such stories end, explosive energy is endorsed.

Again:

Our films are spirals of wish fulfilment, pleas for envy, the hustle to get on with the pursuit of happiness. By contrast, Ozu's films seem to be modeled on novels and plays – Tolstoy or Chekhov – certain that there is no escape, no getting away, and no proper place for fantasy in living.

Like any sane lover of film, I touch wood before I disagree with David Thomson – but isn't American cinema exceptional in this respect, even though it's an exception that has been globally dominant for the best part of a century? It's far the most positive, least self-doubting national cinema (which makes *film noir* such a fascinating anomaly), which may actually be the reason it has become something so much larger than a national cinema, purveyor of wish-fulfilment by appointment to the world.

Hollywood cinema, like the World Series in baseball, lays claim to the planet without particularly noticing it. American films fetishise second chances (any number of them) because the national self-image is of a fresh start, a rebooted Creation with security software in place to screen out the virus of original sin. The notion of a special destiny, an exemption from fate, has proved almost infinitely exportable. America has cornered the market in the ideology of freedom from market forces.

I like the idea of setting up Ozu as a David against the Yankee Goliath, who doesn't even notice the slung stone of subtlety lodged in his forehead (philistine!), but it's much more a case of USA vs. the rest. British films, for instance, tend to rebuke fantasy, or to use it against itself, in genres as different as the love story (*Brief Encounter*), supernatural mystery (*Don't Look Now*) and dystopian satire (*Brazil*, though how I'm going to claim Terry Gilliam as British I haven't yet decided). It's true that British films that do well in the States (*Four Weddings and a Funeral*, *The Full Monty*, even *The Crying Game*) leave space for soft focus. A calculatedly transatlantic product like *Notting Hill* has not only one bankable star from each side of the Atlantic but in effect two endings, the first British and resigned (she was out of your league, it was never going to happen), the second Americanised and self-empowering: give it everything you've got, miracles happen every day! The double ending of *Notting Hill* is like an adaptor allowing the film to plug in smoothly to the local current wherever it is shown.

Not every film is machined to transfer so effortlessly, and films from cultures that are both unfamiliar and over-familiar (in terms of well-worn motifs) pay a price. In particular, when a film is saturated with the imagery of an apparently timeless Japan it can seem to recede emotionally for Western audiences, till all its human urgency drains away. We succumb to a strange loss of peripheral awareness, of all the ways a work of art is linked to its context – call it cherry-blossom blinkers.

It doesn't help that there's quite a tendency in the critical literature to shepherd our gaze gently but firmly towards that transcendent horizon, past the near and middle distance where we would normally spend our time. Consequently the emotions aroused by an Ozu film can remain distinct but isolated, like notes sounded on an exotic instrument (a *koto* perhaps), not connecting up with any familiar tuning or temperament. Feelings in the key of Zen, remote and plinky-plunky, very far from the squelch and murmur of our own hearts.

*Late Spring* starts with a tea ceremony and has an important scene at a performance of a Noh play. Ozu's artistry is agreed to have an exquisite understatement which makes a haiku look hectoring, but let's not rush at transcendence like a Wagyū bull at a gate, at least until we have some idea of what is being transcended. Mystical insight into reality may be the eventual result of immersion in a work of art, if that's the way your sensibility leans, but it's definitely not the place to start. Is the position of a single woman in a rapidly changing society such a bad subject? First the outer diversity, then – if absolutely necessary – the inner unity of all things. Take a look at that opening tea ceremony, for instance. Noriko is in traditional dress, naturally enough (culturally enough). But what's that she's holding? Is it the cloth wallet required to complete her outfit? Nope. It's a handbag. If you can bear to keep your eyes open and not to murmur 'Gosh how Zen' the whole time, you may notice that Noriko is shown from the beginning of the film as belonging to two worlds. The question is whether there is a real place for her in either of them.

The script of *Late Spring*, by the director and Kogo Noda, is based on a short pre-war novel by Kazuo Hirotsu but takes liberties. In the original, the father's pretence of closeness to a woman becomes reality, and no one is left lonely. By making such a drastic turn away from its story line, the script treats the novel as a starting-point merely – not a vase to be contemplated *à la Zen* but treated in a functional, even brusque manner. The screenwriters feel free to tip out faded blooms and stale water so as to present us with a fresh arrangement.

There are other art forms than the cinema of Ozu which make use of a timeless vocabulary of symbols – Golden Age Dutch still-life painting, for instance – but we don't marvel at the hush in quite the same way. We can even see that a vase of tulips is part of a frenzied speculative enterprise, continuous with ship-building and the importation of spices, without losing our pleasure in brushwork and composition.

As an exercise in refreshing the eyesight, consider the original reaction to the arrival of film in

Japan, which was gregarious, almost rowdy, rather than reverent. Ozu's films have become installed as definitively Japanese, but that happened at a particular post-war moment. Perhaps there is more than one Japan, more than one way of being Japanese.

In the early days of cinema in Japan, the 1890s, Western films were screened using the technology of the Cinématographe Lumière and the Edison Vitascope. Admission prices were high (nine cents for general admission, with reductions for students and military, going up to ninety cents for the best seats) but novelty value kept the crowds coming.

Some conventions were carried over from the theatre, where stage machinery was traditionally visible (with scene changes in Kabuki being managed without any equivalent of a curtain being lowered). One early showman arranged the projector on the right-hand side of the stage, the screen on the left. Relatively few of the spectators could see the screen, at least from a useful angle, but they had a good view of the projector. There was a lot more obviously appealing activity going on in that quarter, with a team perhaps a dozen strong working the apparatus.

Richie and Anderson: 'There was a handle-turner to crank the film through the machine, a lens-focuser, a reel-rewinding man, a man to look at the screen and make sure everything was going well, a man to adjust the carbon arcs, a man to thread the machine between reels, a general supervisor, a boy to fan those working round the hot projector, and several others whose duties were not specified.' Special clapping-boards called *hyoshigi*, an inheritance from the Kabuki and Shinga theatres, would be banged to gather the crowd in advance of each new reel to be shown. All this splendid fuss allowed screenings with an actual running time of twenty minutes to stretch out over two or three hours, to everyone's satisfaction.

In Bunraku puppetry there was a role for reciters as well as musicians. They would sit on platforms by the stage, explaining and acting out the drama. In *yose*, the indigenous equivalent of music-hall, there was a different tradition of theatrical story-telling. So it made sense, when audiences were shown one-minute scenes of life abroad, such things being the standard offering in the early days of cinema, for there to be a functionary to explain what was going on. Other countries had similar figures, masters of ceremonies who presided at magic-lantern slide shows and later at showings of films (the French word was *compère*) but in Japan the explainer was enormously popular, and for a long time an indispensable element of cinema-going.

This was the *benshi*. He was on hand to explain to audiences of *The Tsar's Arrival in Paris* that the Tsar of all the Russias was the man tucked away in the carriage and not, as they would have assumed, the one in a far more impressive position on the roof.

The *benshi* would also explain in detail the workings of the projector.

In larger cinemas an orchestral fanfare would announce the entrance of the *benshi*. Members of the audience might call out his name – again a tradition carried over from Kabuki. It was customary, though, for favourite theatre performers to be hailed more or less formally. The new cries of 'Big Mouth' or 'Fish Face' expressed a more unbuttoned relationship between the *benshi* and his audience.

The *benshi* didn't hesitate to intervene between the spectators and what was on the screen. If nothing needed explaining he would weigh in just the same: 'You will kindly note that the smoke comes from the chimney. Also notice dark clouds are in the sky: rain is coming.' (All these lovely details from Richie and Anderson.) Bricks without straw were better than no bricks at all.

In due course (around 1910) a dialogue script for the *benshi* to use was sometimes distributed with a film, but free improvisation seems to have been the norm. It had already come to seem that the same film accompanied by different *benshi* produced quite distinct experiences. Only the characters' names were out of bounds, exempt from variation, almost always Mary for the heroine and Robert for the villain. The knight in shining armour riding to Mary's rescue was almost certain to be Jim.

It wasn't long before the *benshi* had more box-office appeal than the film itself. Even when narrative films and a star system had arrived, advertising would use larger characters for the *benshi* than the ones used for the leading actors, and even for the name of the film. *Benshi* earning power could compete with a top actor's. The distributors didn't find fault with this rather eccentric arrangement, since the system saved them the expense of adding titles to the film.

It was only when the projector broke down that this inflated status had any drawbacks, from the *benshi* point of view. The technical failure reflected badly on him. No one enjoyed being reminded that the powers of the *benshi*, this servant of the film who had mysteriously become its master, began and ended with description.

So the first film culture of Japan, far from thriving on hints and half-tones, had no patience whatever for the implicit and wanted things spelled out with absolute clarity. In other countries there was a drive towards forging a visual grammar for storytelling, but in Japan there was felt to be no need. The *benshi* was always there to fill in the gaps, and his words had a prestige with which images lacking commentary could not compete.

The *benshi* had been a hold-over from theatre conventions, and subtitles in their turn, when eventually they became established, inherited something of the *benshi*'s exhaustive explanatory function. If the film was *Man of a Thousand Faces*, the biographical film about Lon Chaney, who was brought up by deaf parents, then no fragment of sign language, however unimportant in itself, must fall through the net of subtitles. If Jacques Cousteau was showing the wonders of *Le Monde du Silence* to the inhabitants of dry land, then every fish on screen (even in lyrical sequences which dispensed with narration) must be properly identified. When James Stewart as Lindbergh was near the end of his tether in *The Spirit of St Louis*, diligent subtitling drones were busy ('Place de la Concorde', 'Notre Dame', 'Arc de Triomphe') labelling every landmark on the ground.

This institution of the *benshi* had two little episodes of afterlife, once as a self-conscious archaism accompanying the broadcast of silent films on television. Then when *Rashomon* was released domestically, a few superannuated *benshi* came out of retirement to add much-needed clarity, steering audiences dependably, or at least confidently, through an indeterminate narrative.

We in the West have *benshi* of our own, though of course we don't call them that, and Donald Ritchie is undoubtedly one of them. He's entitled, if anyone is. He persuaded Shochiku studios into letting him take five Ozu films to the Berlin Festival in 1963 (not long before Ozu's death). Before then Ozu's only exposure in the West seems to have been a screening of *Their First Trip to Tokyo*, as *Tokyo*

*Story* was called on that occasion, in London in the late 1950s. Even so, Richie's vindicated championing of his favourite shouldn't be allowed to exert a stranglehold on critical response. All his emphasis on the intense, the definitive Japaneseness of Ozu rules out any response but obeisance.

When Donald Richie says in his plot summary of *Late Spring* that Noriko's mother has died 'recently' I don't dismiss the idea, though I don't know the basis for it. There's no dialogue that says so – but if there were subtle signals sent by clothing and by ritual observance then Donald Richie might pick them up and I certainly wouldn't. Logically it would be Noriko's mother who would be expected to take a particular interest in her getting married, and if that side of things has been neglected it may be because she died a considerable time ago, before the subject came up in any pressing form.

When Richie turns Ozu into a religious artist, to be approached only by the initiated, I think he's plain wrong. Sometimes works of art need to be defended against their advocates, and great films rescued from their reputations. Masterpieces are not fragile but robust. They can stand up to more than a reverent dusting.

Any article that tells you What To Look For in an Ozu film also tells you what not to look for, what is guaranteed not to be there, which means anything that connects at all to politics or history.

We're supposed to keep our eyes on the horizon of transcendence.

I'd prefer to be the brash foreigner at the tea ceremony who says, 'As it comes, love, milk and two sugars', rather than the cowed one who pretends to understand but doesn't have a clue. At least the brash one knows that tea is a drink and can satisfy a thirst.

One cultural anomaly was mentioned by Ozu himself, back in 1933 when he was making films strongly influenced by Hollywood (just as there were people who had known Doris Day before she was a virgin, there were audiences who knew Ozu before he was so very Japanese). It's the matter of doors. Doors in the West are hinged, and even in rural communities visitors usually wait to be admitted to the living space. In the Japanese home we see in *Late Spring*, all comers enter without waiting for permission, though bells on the sliding doors announce their presence. There seems to be more than one set of these little bells.

After that there's the formality for everyone, resident or guest, of removing shoes. It's a different rhythm and a different set of assumptions. In 1933 Ozu was advocating that 'the actual Japanese lifestyle should become more cinematic', in other words more American, in preference to Japanese film language adapting to a different tempo of domesticity. This sounds like a tease.

There's a disconcerting moment early in *Late Spring* when the professor is working on a manuscript with his assistant Hattori. The little bells announce a visitor. Up to this point the emphasis has been on the imagery of traditional Japan, at the tea ceremony and also at the professor's house, with its low tables and tatami mats (though Hattori wears a suit). But here is a man come to read the meter [07:35]. He borrows a stool to help him take his reading (it's three kilowatts over), and provides a reminder in passing that this country runs on electricity rather than the rustle of kimonos.

In fact the scene of the professor and his assistant has already contained its own reflection of modernity. The professor's article is about the economist Friedrich List, a contemporary of Marx who was sceptical about cries for free trade when they came from countries which had built up their own economies (as Britain did in the nineteenth century, and America would in the twentieth) by protectionist practices and were now anxious to prevent others from doing the same. This disreputable tactic has become known as 'kicking away the ladder'.

List recommended an individual response to the circumstances of each country's development. His own experiments in capitalism weren't particularly successful, for all the professor's praise (he lost most of his investments and ended a suicide), but that's presumably not the point. In his academic life

Professor Somiya hardly seems to be hiding from the present day. His speciality isn't the history of the *tanka* or the woodblock print but the economics of industrial development.

When the heroine, Noriko (Setsuko Hara), comes home, she serves tea to her father and his assistant but isn't a doormat by any means. Smilingly she vetoes the suggestion of a mah-jong party, on the grounds that work on the article is not yet finished.

It isn't just for her father that she does chores. At the tea ceremony she met her aunt, who mentioned that moths had got at a pair of her husband's striped trousers. Would Noriko be able to mend them? Noriko politely agrees, but reacts with a smothered laugh the moment she realises that her aunt has actually brought the trousers along with her. They're in a nicely wrapped package, as if Noriko was being given a present rather than asked a rather menial favour. Aunt Masa continues to send mixed messages, so that 'don't take too much time on this' is somewhat contradicted by 'reinforce the seat'. The participants at a tea ceremony are supposed to surrender worldly thoughts and observe 'the way of tea' (*chado*), but Aunt Masa sees nothing odd about bringing along some mending to drop off. She lets it be seen that she takes her niece's agreement for granted.

The subtitles don't make it completely clear, but it seems likely that the mended trousers aren't for

Noriko's uncle but for her young cousin Bu-chan. This makes the favour of needlework seem positively demeaning, an outsourced bit of make-do-and-mend, although both branches of the family seem to be prospering.

The next day Noriko goes with her father to Tokyo on the train. She has some shopping to do, as well as a medical appointment. The sequence of the train journey is a famous one, and characteristic in being crisp and loose at the same time. (It might be simpler in the long run to identify the shots in *Late Spring* that aren't famous.) In Hollywood terms this would be an obvious assignment for the second-unit director, since ordinarily images of travel are only there to point up human drama, but it isn't safe to relegate anything to the background of an Ozu film. The visual rhythms are very pleasing.

There's a story that Ozu, when he saw *High Noon* (this would be after he made *Late Spring*), was particularly taken with one shot and decided to imitate it. The shot, part of that film's suspense agenda, showed nothing more than a clock face, but Ozu liked its length, six seconds. This sounds a preposterous thing to borrow, the length of a shot without an interest in what it shows, but it may be that six seconds is somehow a short long shot or a long short one, and lends a distinctive syncopation to a cutting scheme. I don't think this makes Ozu a formalist (someone for whom arbitrary patterns take precedence over mere subject matter), just someone alive to the music of editing.

Ozu's camera seems almost boyishly interested in the train, leaning out of the window to get glimpses of the next carriage. The impression of boyishness is reinforced by the music attached to the sequence, which has a relentless hollow jollity reminiscent of American cartoons of the Thirties and Forties, those Looney Tunes and Merrie Melodies.

This probably doesn't qualify as a travelling shot, since it's the train which is doing the travelling rather than the camera, but there's certainly a feeling of emancipation from stillness. Perhaps Ozu had a soft spot for trains – the first shot of the whole film shows Kamakura station (alternating with empty-shots of nature), and it's doubtful that he's seeking to strip the filmed railway station, as Zen teaching would demand, of all the varieties of expectation attached to it, whether of going to new places or of welcoming visitors, stubbornly rooted associations with adventure or reunion.

I take that back. He does play a game of thwarting expectations with those shots of the station at the very beginning of the film. The suspense is very mild, this isn't remotely *High Noon*, there's just a homoeopathic tingle of anticipation which turns out to be misleading. We hear a train, but don't see one. As far as we know, nobody in the story meets the invisible train or arrives by it. The film breaks the promise of its opening, that the story will get its start from some-one arriving or departing by train. But of course Ozu made no such promise. He didn't even come close. He just hinted, then changed the subject.

The mind, in its rage for coherence, simply lets go of threads that don't spin enough connections for themselves to survive in the memory. It's only when I watch the film again that I remember this odd pro-logue, too significant in its cryptic way to be merely atmospheric. The sly stately drift of images from railway station to tea ceremony is too leisurely to be making a pat point about modernity and tradition.

In human terms the scene on the morning train to Tokyo clarifies the relationship between father and daughter. The train is crowded. At one point he asks her if she'd like to sit – but he asks this from the seat he himself has taken as of right. Presumably this is a concession to her possible status as an invalid (there's that hospital appointment, after all), but in any case she declines his offer. Later there's enough space for them to sit companionably together. So at home she is playful and spirited, though ministering to her father's needs throughout, but in public space there are no troubling signs of a Westernised will running rampant.

One shot from the train sequence is an exam-ple of Ozu's idiosyncratic approach to continuity. Father and daughter are in conversation, but the camera shows us their intercut heads aligned in the same direction, facing the right of the screen. It takes a moment to realise that the landscape outside the window is moving in the 'wrong' direction behind the father, and that 'in reality' the two of them are facing each other. Of course there is no 'reality' to be appealed to, only actors doing what they have been told. It's just that Ozu disregards the convention, unchallengeable in Hollywood films (usually known as the 180° rule), that cutting doesn't disorientate the viewer in this way.

What is interesting, though, is not how destabilising the discontinuity is, but how easily ignored. As if this was the equivalent in film of a printing error, audiences rapidly work out what was 'meant', and then forget that there was ever any doubt about it.

'Continuity' in cinema normally means consistency of exactly this sort, so that an impression of solidity can be built up by the mutually corroborating testimony of actors, sets and objects, but you could also say that the basic operation of the art form depends on the illusion of continuity, used in a slightly different sense – perhaps 'continuousness' expresses the idea better. What flickers in front of the eyes is a rapid succession of images, which the brain stitches together into a continuous flow.

This phenomenon is usually referred to as the persistence of vision, but that seems too passive a description of the way the brain works, the tireless spinneret secreting the spider-silk of coherence. A film like *Late Spring* refuses coherence on a number of levels, but we can't help tidying the loose ends away. And of course we aren't aware of doing the tidying. The fact of tidying up is tidied away in its turn.

In Ozu's group scenes, such as the tea ceremony early in *Late Spring*, it's hard to be sure how many people are present, since they don't 'keep still' between shots, as classical Hollywood film language requires. We're not offered a stable tableau inspected from different angles but a fluid arrangement. Of course classic American cinema has plenty of tricks to play, but those tricks, even when they undermine the viewer's privileged position, work by establishing it first. In Ozu's films there's something closer to an uncertainty principle at work.

One scene in *Late Spring* seems to comment on this stylistic quirk of Ozu's with considerable playfulness. A visitor to the professor's house asks him about the location of various landmarks of the neighbourhood. Is the sea over there? And how about the shrine? And Tokyo? He points in various directions and is wrong in every case. The professor points a finger authoritatively to set him right – but each time he does so, the camera cuts to another angle, disrupting the reassurance of stable orientation. I dare say it's possible to pause the DVD shot by shot (something Ozu could hardly have foreseen) and to build up a satisfactory mental picture of the house in its environment, even at a pinch an architect's model, but the immediate effect is to make sure that the viewer's compass needle is spinning at least as wildly as the visitor's.

Admittedly the film's geography isn't always so indeterminate. The train's arrival in Tokyo is signalled by two emphatic shots (from different angles) of the Hattori building, a landmark in its own right, one which happens to share its name with the professor's assistant. Kristin Thompson in her notable book *Breaking The Crystal Armor* (subtitled 'neoformalist film analysis'), sees this as an example of superfluous information thwarting the narrative flow, drawing attention away from human drama and towards patterns of formal play. The effect, as she sees it, is the equivalent of using two rather overemphatic shots of Big Ben (filmed from different angles, so that they can hardly represent a single individual's experience) to say 'London'.

Ozu attracts these rather extreme readings, and the history of his films' reception in the West has been a sort of tug-of-war between the Zen transcendentals, with Paul Schrader at their head, and neoformalists like Thompson and her husband David Bordwell. For both camps the films are apolitical, indifferent to history except as it impinges on family relations. I wonder, though. It seems more than a coincidence that *Late Spring* is agreed to announce the arrival of Ozu's mature style, and is exhaustively analysed on that basis, when he made other post-war films before it (*Record of a Tenement Gentleman* in 1947, *Hen in the Wind* in 1948) which confront their period directly. In *Hen in the Wind*, for instance, a soldier returning home from the war finds that his wife has resorted to prostitution to survive.

'Resorted to prostitution' puts it a bit high, though that is how a number of accounts describe it, since she has sold herself a single time, in order to buy medicine for her sick son. Her husband himself forces her sexually and at one stage pushes her downstairs, and though, yes, there is a mood acceptance by the time the story works itself out, the film isn't exactly a happy hunting-ground for either the Zen merchants or the pattern obsessives.

In Tokyo Noriko has a chance meeting with a family friend called Onodera (she addresses him as 'uncle'). They do some shopping together, and end up in a bar where Onodera drinks *sake*. He asks if she'd like some, but the modernity of her behaviour stops short of that indulgence, though she's happy to pour the flask for him.

The main part of their conversation is very odd. Noriko mentions that she has heard Onodera has remarried, and she uses a whole series of disparaging terms for what he has done, but she never stops smiling. At first it's possible to think that she's teasing him, but her condemnation is too specific to be put on. First of all she claims to feel sorry for Onodera's daughter, saying it's not 'natural'. She's deprived of this fantasy ally when Onodera says that Isako doesn't mind. From then on, Noriko speaks on her own account, without using a decoy for her disapproval. 'I'd find it distasteful.'

'Distasteful? My new wife?'

'No, you, uncle.'

'Why?'

'It seems filthy.'

'Filthy?'

'It's foul.'

He tries to steer the conversation towards banter, and he's certainly indulgent rather than angry, but this is hardly small talk. One idea in the critical literature is that remarriage in traditional Japanese culture (for women above all, but also for men) was seen as an offence against the existing family, but that doesn't seem to apply here. If Isako doesn't mind, why should Noriko? In any case, if Noriko was so attached to the traditional ways she would hardly be so forward as to start a conversation on the subject. She has been relaxed enough with Onodera to tolerate a joke of his about a pigeon soiling a statue, and she invites him home to her father's for more *sake*, an odd way of expressing disapproval.

When the professor comes home the men have a certain amount of serious conversation over their *sake*. Then Onodera brings up the subject of his status as a sinner in Noriko's eyes. He repeats the words she used earlier, teasingly pressing her to confirm his pariah status. She says in mild disarray, 'Oh, I don't know!' and retreats to the kitchen. Perhaps she is embarrassed by the presence of her father, an unforceful character but still the source of the household's authority, for having spoken so plainly to his friend. Certainly this recapitulation of the theme of sexual disgust is in a lighter key.

If there's one thing the actress playing Noriko, Setsuko Hara, is known for, it's her smile. It's the key to her mystique. This is a facial expression that seems to come from the depths, not something put on for the purposes of social appeasement, yet it doesn't necessarily have strong links with happiness or even contentment. The 'Noriko smile' is a filmed entity which obeys its own laws, like Chaplin's little-tramp walk or Fred Astaire's way with a song.

The Noriko smile doesn't appear exclusively in *Late Spring*. There are two other Ozu films with characters of the same name played by the same actress, *Early Summer* (1951) and *Tokyo Story* (1953), but it's stretching a point to call them a 'trilogy', as many critics do, when the stories don't form any kind of unity, variously overlapping and contradicting each other.

The lack of fit between facial expression and overall mood isn't exclusively a female phenomenon. When the professor and Onodera discuss a serious topic, it's with any number of grins and chuckles.

Do we need to come up with a theory of the Japanese smile, as a cultural construct differing from anything in the West? Donald Richie thinks so, to judge by the last section of his 1987 book *Different People*. He sees someone he knows by sight, the wife of the local tofu man, missing her train.

Mrs Watanabé stopped short in front of the closed doors now sliding past and smiled. At a moment when we of the West would have turned our mouths down, she turned hers up. It was not an ironic grimace, common enough, nor was it mock despair for the benefit of those looking on. The smile was innocent and natural enough to seem instinctive.

But what kind of instinct could create this expression of delight, I wondered. And what assumptions lie behind it? This was not the first such smile I had seen. I saw it daily, on the faces of those apparently pleased to have missed the train. The tofu man's wife was simply the latest in a long line of disappointed grinners.

I can't help noticing that a grin is not a smile, is almost the opposite of a smile, and also that an implausibly unanimous Western grimace has been posited ('when we of the West would have turned our mouths down') to balance the similarly communal Japanese facial expression.

Donald Richie characterises Mrs Watanabé's culturally resonant smile more fully: it is 'wide and forbearing, with only a trace of self-consciousness or embarrassment'. It testifies, according to him, to a belief that acceptance outranks irritation. Harmony is more important than discord, and individual priorities must yield to communal ones.

He admits that a culture which learns this lesson over centuries becomes easy to manipulate, but finds that he envies Mrs Watanabé's 'beautiful, indulgent smile' just the same. (The beauty and the indulgence are new ideas, introduced by sleight of hand. Who or what is being indulged?) He ends with the familiar Zen cadences of acceptance, referring to the proper attitude of the haiku master and, yes, Ozu, not to mention 'how the true Zen *roshi* approaches the real and instant now'. By this point in Donald Richie's life he had known Japan for four decades, and still he seems to be wearing the cherry-blossom blinkers. What he describes as a beautiful, indulgent, wide and forbearing smile sounds like the opposite of a personal expression, something more like the serene mask that women (particularly) in many cultures are trained to produce.

I don't know many Japanese proverbs – in fact I only know one. Luckily it's this one: the face smiles, while the heart cries.

But let's keep our eyes on the screen, shall we? If there's a Noriko smile in the film there is also an Aunt Masa smile, though perhaps 'grin' really is the word here. She wears a harsh lopsided smirk of satisfaction when her plans to marry off her niece begin to come near their fulfilment. She emits a self-righteous, almost punitive glow.

Aunt Masa is only ever seen in traditional dress, but she does an odd job of maintaining the standards of Old Japan. In her first conversation with her brother, before the discussion of marriage starts to focus on Noriko, she refers to a wedding the two of them recently attended, at which the bride drank *sake*. Masa's disgust is phobic, almost sexual in its intensity, and centres on the bride's wearing lipstick as well as publicly indulging in food and drink, separate improprieties made much worse in combination. Lipstick on *sashimi* – ugh!

Somiya teases her, saying that if Masa herself was getting married in these modern times, she wouldn't refuse food either. He makes excuses for the bride, saying her behaviour was understandable. 'We hadn't had that for a long time,' he says. The freshly rendered subtitles, 'new and improved', of the British Film Institute's version of *Late Spring* (released in 2010 as the first instalment of an Ozu Collection) spell things out a bit more. Now what the professor says is 'We haven't been able to get it for a long time.' He's referring to the deprivations of war and its aftermath, though I still don't know which has been the unavailable luxury, as between lipstick or *sashimi*.

The new subtitles on the BFI version don't make important changes to the meaning of the film, though they're fuller, translating for instance what's written on posters. I give the wordings of the Tartan

Video subtitles, if only because that's the version I watched first, and also the frame references that apply to that release.

Why the two sets of timings should diverge, I've no idea – at this point in the dialogue between Somiya and Masa, though we're already at minute 24:54 of Tartan time, it's only 23:27 by the BFI's stopwatch. By the end of *Late Spring*, the Tartan version has logged over four minutes more than the BFI's. It's a shame that giving frame timings to the second, with a precision of reference that promises to put mere page numbers in the shade, should turn out to be so tricky. I doubt if there's something about *Late Spring* that refuses to be pinned down, but in that respect it couldn't happen to a better film. If you're watching the BFI version, you'll have to subtract roughly a twentieth from the figures I give. Good luck!

So Masa claims to derive her morality from tradition. But does her own behaviour measure up? On a visit to a shrine with her brother, she finds a wallet someone has left behind. (The subtitles call it a wallet, though to Western eyes it resembles an old-fashioned woman's purse, the sort with a rigid top edge that clicks open and shut.) She tells the professor that this is a good omen that the proposed marriage will take place. He points out that it is her duty to hand the wallet in to the authorities, and she agrees but says there's no hurry.

Later on, when Noriko gives in to pressure and

agrees to the marriage, Aunt Masa is exultant, saying 'That wallet did it!' She pats it where it nestles inside her traditional costume. The professor is dismayed that she's still hanging on to someone else's property, and again she reassures him that of course she will be handing it in. We hear no more about it in the film, but there's nothing to indicate that Masa is being sincere about doing the right thing. Behind that traditional costume, behind those censorious attitudes, beats a pilferer's heart.

Before Aunt Masa's scheming gets under way, there is one quite significant piece of narrative manipulation. Noriko goes on a bicycle trip to the countryside with her father's assistant Hattori. The atmosphere is relaxed, even exhilarated, and the bicycle functions as much as a marker of freedom and romantic possibility as it does in *Jules et Jim*. The slightly heightened mood makes Hattori seem a real prospect as a husband for her.

There's some Ozu eccentricity in the way the bicycle outing is filmed. In (dare I say?) reality the two young people are riding side by side, but he films them separately and edits them together so that one moves across the screen from left to right, the other from right to left. In Hollywood film language, this would indicate that they were riding towards each other on a collision course – but even hardened Western audiences don't need special training to tell them that this is not a possible interpretation.

It's only for a subliminal instant that it looks as if Noriko and Hattori are playing a demure two-wheeled version of the 'chicken' game from *Rebel Without a Cause*.

As they cycle along side by side, Noriko makes sure her hair is in place with one hand. This is a fairly meaningless piece of primping since her hair is being agitated by the breeze and the speed of her travel, but it seems fair to take it as a sign that she's keen to make a good impression. It's more than a routine nervous gesture, since she has to take one hand off the handlebars to reassure herself that her grooming will pass muster.

In 1949 the theme of man and woman was not new, the possibilities of solitude and a beach were not new, and the film's first audiences must have been expecting a scene of romance, perhaps even (though this would have been a first for Ozu) a scene of kissing. There is a shot of the two bicycles propped up on their stands, side by side near the sand dunes, which has a delicate sub-erotic frisson. Clearly the people who were riding these bicycles have wandered away from their mechanical chaperones. Perhaps they too are respectably upright, and perhaps not. The shot is held long enough for us to wonder. Cinema didn't get where it is today by discouraging low speculation.

Admittedly the music, every bit as oppressively jaunty as the music for the train sequence, hardly promotes a charged atmosphere. It seems to be paying homage to the Woody Woodpecker theme tune.

Back in 1946 spring had taken a new turn, when along with the timeless recurrence of blossom, cherry and plum, there was a sudden flowering of kisses to be seen on the cinema screens of Japan.

Before then, there had been no kisses in Japanese films and the ones in foreign ones were cut out. Continuity was violated as a matter of course. In the prints as they reached the cinemas, lovers would move together passionately and then spring apart before they embraced, as if the romantic encounter created a rift in time, the lips moving towards union composed of matter and anti-matter, fated to cancel each other out in the intimacy of a self-abolishing event.

The historic first kiss in Japanese cinema bears the date of May 23, 1946. One director (Yasukie Chiba) had announced the breakthrough in the very title of his new film, *A Certain Night's Kiss*, then lost his nerve, inserting an open umbrella to obscure the controversial element of the shot, the actual collision of mouths. Yasushi Sasaki held steady with *Twenty-Year-Old Youth* and delivered the unprecedented image.

There followed a modest vogue, though there was still a certain amount of shying away from physical fact. Kissing scenes might still be faked, filmed from an angle which made it impossible for audiences to tell that the partners in passion were hardly even touching cheeks. There might be elaborate make-up schemes, the sort of thing which in Hollywood would be used for the staging of violence (blanks, prostheses, squibs of blood): gauze over both sets of lips retouched with make-up, so as to make possible both a symbolic union and an actual quarantine. The qualms weren't exactly consistent, since Richie and Anderson mention a film (*Brilliant Revenge*) which included a kiss on stage without embarrassment. The actors in the play within that film were nominally foreigners, although played by Japanese, and it was well known that foreigners kiss all the time, whatever the audience.

The young people in the seaside scene from *Late Spring* aren't upright, when we see them at last, but they are respectable. There is no great closeness of faces, though the relaxation of Noriko's posture is a little surprising. Hattori sits down on a tufted sand dune and Noriko sits beside him, but her upper body goes some little way towards the horizontal. She leans back, taking her weight on her hands. Then instead of any sort of intimacy we get a long and excruciating scene of banter on the subject of pickles – pickles and jealousy. We start in the middle of things. She says, 'Then which type do you say I am?', as if there had already been a discussion of 'types'.

So *he* says, 'Well, you're not the jealous type.'
Then *she* says, 'On the contrary, I am.'

And *he* says, 'I wonder.'

*She* says, 'Pickles stick together when I cut them. It means I'm jealous.'

*He* says, 'That's only a matter of the knife and cutting board. There's no connection between pickles and jealousy.'

You'd think the pickles-and-jealousy theme (all delivered as if it was the most sparkling dialogue ever thought of) had been done to death. But no. *She* says, 'So, do you like pickles stuck together?'

*He* says, 'That's fine, sometimes.'

*She* says, 'Really?'

Stop it at once, young people. Not another word about pickles. Not another word about jealousy. Tear each other's clothes off if you must (though the camera won't know where to look). Just give the cryptic kitchen banter a rest.

The obvious assumption to make would be that pickle talk was all the rage among young people in post-war Japan, so that the excessive obliqueness of this dialogue is simply a matter of our angle of vision. Stop, Yukio – this pickle talk is burning my lips! This chatting is truly spicy.

But what if that isn't the case? The references are obscure to modern Japanese audiences, and perhaps they always were. The best explanation anyone has been able to come up with is that the pickles in question are large and thick-skinned, and therefore require a strong confident stroke of the knife if a slice is to be fully separated from the mother pickle. So if you're distracted, by reason of jealousy or (let's face it) any number of other reasons, then the pickles 'stick together', with the slices remaining residually attached.

I wonder if Ozu isn't just being playful, saying in effect: you want a love scene? Fine, but you're going to have to do the work. And you have to build it out of pickles. All the best! I'll leave you to it.

When we last see the two young people on their trip to the seaside, they are walking away from those respectably upright bicycles, which leaves open the possibility of a less cryptic intimacy off camera. They almost seem to be falling in step with each other. Noriko tucks her left hand, the one nearer Hattori, behind her back, as if she was suppressing the urge to reach out towards him with it.

Neoformalist criticism, as adroitly practised by Kristin Thompson, calls attention to the Coke sign visible in the scene on the way to the beach. The term she uses for this is 'hypersituated', standing outside the narrative – after all, there's nowhere on the beach to buy a bottle of soda, and no one in the film seems to drink it. There's another English-language sign in the scene, certifying the load capacity of a bridge, but Thompson doesn't mention it.

Perhaps this would be a good time to express the necessary amazement at the critical reception of Ozu's post-war cinema, as represented by *Late*

*Spring*. No one seems to find it strange that film critics, both Japanese and American, should choose these works as icons of depth and integrity. Perhaps the logic is that they embody an inner Japan, since they so plainly don't represent an outer one.

If there's a Coke sign on a Japanese beach in 1949, it's because more than a third of a million American personnel were billeted on the country at the time. Donald Richie presumably knows this, since he was one of them. If the Coke sign bears on its post an arrow indicating HIRATSUKA BEACH then it's because English speakers without Japanese language skills are no less entitled to be directed to the amenities. If there's a sign on a bridge in English announcing that it is safe for loads up to 30 tons, then that's because a victorious army needs the information for the safe deployment of its tanks and trucks, the heavy machinery of occupation.

A true portrait of post-war Japan would have to show the American presence, but then film production was hardly free. In this context, that Coke sign, that certification of the bridge's tolerance, are the most oblique of allusions to American influence. Could we perhaps say that it is the American occupation, rather than the Coke sign, which is 'hyper-situated' in the text of *Late Spring* – not part of the narrative but claiming a place nonetheless, by virtue of what it permits and forbids in the world of the story.

It must have seemed, to a cinema industry needing to watch its step, that the best options were going backwards, into the far past, or inwards, to the
intimacy of the family drama, where Westernisation
is a subtler force. Against the background of the distant past, as in Mizoguchi's period dramas, recent
upheavals could be replayed in all their pain. The
scene in *Ugetsu Monogatari* (1953) where the pot-
ter's wife is stabbed almost unnoticeably, her faint
expiring sounds drowned by the cries of her child,
while the beggars who have half-accidentally killed
her squabble over the pitiful supply of food she was
carrying, was presumably a lot closer to the recent
experience of its audiences, despite the patina of
period, than anything in Ozu.

The scene at the beach, romantic but not very,
is a sort of narrative Rorschach blot – is that the
answer to a maiden's prayer or just a pickle in the
shape of a heart? It reveals genre expectations rather than fulfils them. There's some confirmation of
this idea after Hattori has left. Noriko's father is very
interested in the young people's little trip, once he
is reassured that they didn't share a bicycle. Relax,
professor – Hattori brought his own, and she borrowed one from somewhere. There was no brushing
of hand against hand on the handlebars, and it was
separate saddles all the way. But there's no denying
the exhilaration of an outing in slacks.

Delicately he sounds her out on her feelings for

the young man. She talks about Hattori's gentleness, and the professor, encouraged, asks point-blank whether he might be a good marriage prospect for her. She seems highly amused, and tells him that Hattori is engaged already, to a very nice girl. Noriko knows her well – they know each other from school.

On the Richter scale of cinematic shock, with John Hurt's tummy upset in *Alien* scoring 7.8 and the shower scene from *Psycho* clocking in at a solid 8.6, this revelation rates no more than 1.2. Barely enough to make a chandelier tinkle. But it does make the point that we see what we expect to see. Ozu can't really be accused of breach of promise. Nothing had led us to expect a love scene at the beach except the whole history of cinema.

The bicycle-and-beach sequence is certainly given energy by some mild subversion of genre, but perhaps it has another point to make. Ozu's mystique, either as Zen master or neoformalist pattern-maker, is so strong that it seems almost blasphemous to suggest he may be constructing sequences as it were classically, with strategic management of effects and a larger purpose in mind.

What is established in the beach sequence, though disguised by the information which is withheld and then sprung as a small surprise? Perhaps that Noriko can be relaxed, intimate, even playful with a man as long as there is no sexual implication. Since the whole later course of the film is shaped by

Noriko's resistance, the scene on the beach has the useful function of showing that she can have warm feelings for a man near her own age. (Some assessments of the film make out that she is over-attached to her father in a way that amounts to emotional incest, an 'Electra complex', which seems to me a very distorted account both of her spirited dealings with her father and her relaxation with Hattori.) If marriage repels her, then perhaps another factor is involved.

The little shock of Hattori's unavailability isn't there for its own sake. It's set up as a piece of misdirection, and the point of misdirection is to convey something while the audience's attention is bounced elsewhere. In a conjuring context this would be the rabbit slipped into the hat. Here some information about Noriko's character is slipped into the unattended back part of the viewer's awareness.

In Henry James's version of a widower and daughter who form a sort of couple, Adam and Maggie Verver in *The Golden Bowl*, there's much more potential for claustrophobia. Both Ververs marry, of course, although the new relationships which were supposed to dissolve their interdependence end up merely complicating it. The comparison of Ozu to James is a fairly standard bit of critical business, though I can't be alone in finding James's obliqueness portentous and even overbearing. Reading his later novels I long for something closer to Ozu's fluidity.

In *Late Spring* it's only when Aunt Masa gets in

on the act that marriage acquires the status of an oppressive fate. In the discussion between Noriko and her father there is no particular tension. Noriko enjoys deflating her father's expectations – but Aunt Masa has a suitable prospect in mind, and wants Noriko at least to meet him. This seems reasonable enough in its way, but from that point onward Noriko must struggle to keep the place in life she has already achieved.

Her life is far from being unbalanced. She looks after her father but has a significant amount of independence. She can socialise freely, and has an unsupervised life outside the home. If her way of life with her father sometimes resembles a marriage (as is often mentioned in the critical literature) rather than a parent-child relationship, surely that is because of its parity – not in fact a hallmark of the traditional Japanese marriage. The commentators who see her as somehow playing the role of spouse may be importing alien criteria of wifeliness. Symmetrical intimacy is historically an unusual ideal of marriage. It is hardly likely that Noriko's mother, that melancholy shade, had a life so tailored to her personality, so expressive of her needs.

Downstairs, sharing the space with her father, Noriko may sit on a *tatami* mat, though there is Western furniture visible too. Her room upstairs is furnished with bentwood chairs, so that life can be lived at some continuous distance from the floor.

When Noriko is put under pressure as a guest in Aunt Masa's house, her resistance is clearly expressed as a struggle between bodily postures. Masa, in traditional costume, wants her to go on sitting on the mat, and to accept the guidance of her elders in the traditional way. To assert your own preferences and to rise from the *tatami* mat are two aspects of the same agenda. Before Noriko can say No she must free herself of the submissiveness expressed by the traditional posture.

To me this scene, despite the alleged uneventfulness of Ozu's cinema, is an action sequence of an intense and specialised sort. Whether or not Masa is consciously manipulating the conventions Noriko is trying to escape, she responds in the same twofold way. Rather than contesting her niece's arguments, she concentrates on willing Noriko back to her position on the mat. The bowed head of a respectable woman, her bent knees, these attitudes preserve as physical memory a thousand accumulating acts of self-negation. If the aunt is an enemy, then so is the mat, saturated as it is with female sacrifice. Noriko is taking on the combined forces of family pressure and culturally impregnated furnishings.

The scene starts with Masa putting on her apron, the samurai armour of the domineering housewife. She is sending the message that the conversation to come, so fiercely consequential, is no more than a casual chat carried on while she's engaged in the more important activity of housework. It also signifies that she is engaged on a more abstract sort of tidying, putting her house (her family) in order, brushing away the cobwebs in the corners, those loose threads connecting father and daughter who don't properly belong together any more.

When Masa raises the crucial subject, saying 'Isn't it time for you to get married?', Noriko responds with the greatest casualness. 'Oh, that?' she says, 'please leave it,' and rises to her feet. This is clearly a more drastic project when you're starting from ground level than it is in a culture where people in relaxed social space are already halfway to the vertical. In fact it could hardly be more daunting, under the eyes of a bossy aunt, except possibly in cultures where the neutral position of social life is lying face down on the floor.

Masa soon tames her down to mat level again ('I won't leave it. Sit down.'). This first effort to escape was altogether too ambitious. Noriko accomplished the would-be dismissive movement with her usual grace, but it was naive of her to think that an unwelcome concern like marriage would simply tumble from her lap, like a napkin, the moment she stood up.

Masa steps up the pressure by saying, 'I have a fine prospect. Won't you meet him?'

Aunt Masa may be backward-looking, but she isn't benighted. She understands that a prospective husband's looks are part of the bargain proposed, and does her best to do justice to them. Not only is Satake a graduate of Tokyo University with a golden future at Nitto Chemicals ('just right for you, and his office speaks highly of him'), he bears a facial resemblance to Gary Cooper, 'especially his mouth . . . but not the top half'. In such an assessment the viewer's imaginary attention (presumably Noriko's also) is drawn to the qualification following the flattering likeness, the facial area which doesn't measure up – not like Gary Cooper but not like anyone or anything else, a blank space in the metaphysical Photofit.

Noriko's next attempt to defy the familial pressure is more oblique, even strategic. First she lays down a smokescreen, saying, 'I don't want to get married yet.'

'Not yet? Why?'

'Well . . . there will be problems if I get married.'

'What is it?'

'My father. You know, I'm used to it . . . but he can be very difficult. If I leave him alone he'll be in trouble.' This is pretty flimsy as a distracting manœuvre, since the person in question may be the mildest father, not just in Japanese cinema, but in the whole history of film. It's also not a line likely to convince an aunt, someone who knew the person being referred to before you were even born.

Nevertheless the rhetorical diversion enables Noriko to rise from the mat and seat herself in a cane chair instead – for even Aunt Masa the traditionalist has Western furniture alongside the Japanese. From her new vantage point Noriko looks out of the window and says, 'I'm the one who understands him best.'

Before she undertook this quietly dramatic diagonal gambit she lowered her eyes, as is only right for a dutiful niece, but then changed the meaning of her averted gaze by not looking at Masa while she moved to the chair. The initial breaking of eye contact was done in a respectful manner, but there is nothing respectful about looking out of the window while she speaks in the presence of an older family member. In the strangulated vocabulary of women's revolt in such a culture this is strong stuff, defiance as close to direct as can be tolerated even for a moment.

The furniture is more than mere supporting cast, and it continues to shape the action taking place around it. There are tables as well as chairs – the low square Japanese table between the women at the beginning of the confrontation (I almost feel I should draw a battle plan), and a higher round cane table matching the chair where Noriko sits. It was at the low table, its straight edges conforming to a rigid social geometry, that Noriko was challenged (almost arraigned) by Masa on the marriage question. Now she has found a outpost with a different set of assumptions, and can look obliquely away from her aunt without contradicting the furniture.

Masa is clever enough not to dispute Noriko's claim to understand her father best, and to keep the focus on her own priorities. 'Leave him out of this,' she says. 'How about yourself?'

She says, 'I don't want to do it like that,' and only then turns to meet Masa's eyes.

'Then you can never get married.'

'I don't mind.' She smiles.

Of course the crisis isn't over. There follows a moment of false calm, in which both women resort to routines of displacement behaviour. Each is pretending in her own way that this is not a crucial discussion. So Noriko picks up a stray thread from the round table-top and starts playing with it idly. This is a 'relaxed' gesture of the kind designed to manufacture the ease it simulates. Noriko is in particular need of gathering her forces because this meeting has been engineered to take place away from the professor's house. Aunt Masa has the territorial advantage. Noriko is away from her home turf and must guard against being undermined while deprived of the psychological reinforcements of home.

Meanwhile Masa produces a cloth that hasn't been visible before now and starts wiping the square table, as if hoping to summon up some genie of female duty from that gleaming surface. It may be that her niece's resistance has been fiercer than she expected, but Masa has a secret weapon ready, gleaming in readiness like the polished table.

The whole sequence at Masa's house started deceptively, with Noriko upstairs half-comforting, half-teasing her young cousin Bu-chan, who was in a sulk. Then Masa called her downstairs, saying her guest was just leaving. Noriko went down and greeted this person, an elegant lady she had seen before, with all politeness. That was the point (once they were alone) when Masa put on her apron and got to work with her grand tidying project.

Now she says, 'Noriko, that Mrs Miwa you've just met . . . how about her for your father?'

'What do you mean?'

'Your father will need someone if you're not here. I was wondering if she would do.' Noriko has been outmanœuvred here, if not stitched up like a kipper.

Masa is confident enough now to break the spell of cane chair and round table. 'Come here,' she says. 'Sit down.' Noriko reluctantly realigns herself with the charged grid of traditional furniture. She sits down on the mat facing the camera, on the other side of the low table from where she was before.

Aunt Masa goes on, 'She had a good husband but, poor her, he died, leaving her with no children. What do you think? She's a sound woman with good taste.'

For the second time in the sequence Noriko

breaks eye contact with her aunt, but the effect is entirely different. Her eyes slide off to one side. When she was sitting at the round table she could orient the world according to her own compass-rose. Wherever she looked was due north, and her aunt's plans could be rendered tangential, irrelevant, not even needing to be contradicted. Now she has no choice but to sit directly opposite Masa, and sooner or later she will have to meet her eyes. The body language catalysed by the furniture now seems more appropriate to a thwarted child than an autonomous adult.

She asks, 'Does Father know about this?'

'I did mention it to him.'

Noriko is still playing with the thread she found on the table, but all pretence of relaxaton has fallen away. She winds it tightly round her finger.

'What did he say?'

'He was polishing his pipe, but he didn't object.'

Noriko looks up, coldly by her standards. 'Then why do you need my opinion?'

'But I need to know how you feel about it.'

Noriko's face is fixed but also defeated. She says, 'It's up to him, isn't it?' and the music starts which will take us across to the next scene.

The confrontation at Masa's house isn't famous as the Kyoto vase is famous, or as the Noh play sequence is famous, but for me it's the heart of *Late*

*Spring*. But then it isn't a rule that a film can have only the one heart. It may be that any work of art that outlives its original audience is reaping the benefits of polycardism.

Perhaps this scene escapes notice because it is narrative and apparently naturalistic, while the legend of Ozu directs our attention to other styles and registers. The tension here rises steadily without ever leaving the domain of the low-key. It's a deafening murmur. In a medium where melodrama is standard currency, intensity of this sort, not boosted by imposed dynamics or artificial crises, can pass for ordinary. It's the quiet ones you have to watch.

Eventually Noriko agrees to meet the marriage prospect whose office speaks so highly of him. The film never shows us this man, not even when he has been promoted to fiancé and finally to groom. Ozu's decision not to show him is a strong one, throwing all the emphasis on Noriko and her negative impulses, leaving us enclosed in her state of mind without the options of contradiction (he seems nice) or crude corroboration (Gary Cooper my arse!). Perhaps from her point of view, and certainly from ours, since we haven't had so much as a glimpse, the issue is not the particular match but the general category of marriage. What it entails. What is required by it.

The issue of marriage is reduced to its bare bones, not just by the film's removal of any characteristics the groom might have, but also by the non-appearance of one of the strongest arguments traditionally brought in favour of the institution, the possibility of children. The season of the heroine's life may be late spring, but there is no reference to the prospect of harvest. It's easy to imagine that Masa would harp on this theme. Depriving her of a trump card is perhaps not realistic (and Noriko, to judge by her conversations with her nephew, has no aversion to children as a class). There must be an advantage to be gained by this simplification – perhaps that, if children were mentioned as a benefit, then Professor Somiya might seem to have selfish motives as well as altruistic ones for wanting to see Noriko married, the desire for grandchildren and the continuation of family.

As it is, the pressures brought to bear on Noriko, from Aunt Masa and her father, aren't quite symmetrical enough to be described as a pincer movement. They squash her, but without precise co-ordination. Masa's motivation is her love of the proprieties energised by the joy of meddling, while the professor sends misleading signals only with the intention of removing himself from the equation altogether. His thinking is that Noriko, believing that he will have someone to look after him, will listen to her own desires at last, and act on them.

Presumably the professor plays along with Masa's match-making plans for him simply to give Noriko a nudge towards her own independent future. Referring to the climactic scene at a performance of Noh drama, in which the professor nods to Mrs Miwa, a mild social acknowledgement which is enough to plunge Noriko into turmoil, Keiko I. McDonald remarks (in *Reading a Japanese Film*) that 'a less worried daughter would have seen that the Noh meant much more to her father than the lady across the way'. This is perfectly true, except that its lack of sympathy renders it meaningless in human terms. Just as true, and much more to the point, would be to say that a more observant father would have realised that no taint of rancour or martyrdom spoils Noriko's ease and happy functioning in his home. Why should he feel the need to spoil his own happiness, in the name of a fantasy of marital fulfilment which his daughter clearly doesn't share?

The professor may sincerely want Noriko to have a life of her own, but he does a shockingly poor job of selling her on the prospect. Late on in the process, with the cultural conveyor-belt well on its way to tipping her into the marriage-bed, he says to Noriko, 'Your mother wasn't happy at the start. We had our troubles for years. I found her weeping in the kitchen so many times . . .' This must qualify as the worst pep-talk ever. Belatedly he seems to catch on to the bleak tone of what he's saying, and manages a marginally more upbeat ending: 'But your mother put up with me. You must have faith and love each other.'

What he can't take back, because it's part of the overall design of the film, is the fact that this is the only discussion of the dead woman. She becomes an emblem of marital unhappiness, and the professor, whatever his conscious intentions, seems to be prophesying years of tears in the kitchen for someone who has experienced her domestic life to date as serene.

As a consequence of the fluid mechanics of Ozu's approach to film-making, nothing is altogether tidied away. His style is often described as ascetic and uncluttered, as if it was the cinematic equivalent of a minimalist Japanese interior – but such an approach to the running of a home always requires some kind of box room where things can be stored when not in use. His peculiar talent is for leaving the door of that box room half-open, now and then, so that a certain amount of disorder can be glimpsed.

Hattori, who has been eliminated so conclusively as a love object, pops out of his box. To reach the second (and last) of his scenes with Noriko I have to wind back my account of the film, back to a stage in its unfolding when the idea of marriage has been bruited but not strongly pushed on the heroine. Aunt Masa is on manœuvres, to be sure, but only covert ones. The campaign hasn't been formally launched (with the scene at Masa's house), let alone opened up on two fronts by her father's pose of complicity in Masa's plans. Noriko can still treat the subject of marriage humorously. It's something that hasn't yet taken on the meaning of a threat to her security.

The two young people meet in the Balboa Tea and Coffee shop. Again the Hattori building announces the location as 'Tokyo', but just the once this time. Ozu doesn't allow hypersituation (if that's what it is) to become a tic. The tone of easy banter carries over from the scene on the beach, though Noriko takes a rather cynical line on marriage and its associated rituals. She asks Hattori what wedding present he would like (he says that from the professor he'd like something to keep) and she specifies a price range – between two and three thousand yen – as if that was the important thing, the shell of the gift not its personal significance, the element of social performance and class display.

Hattori mentions that he has a spare ticket for a concert that evening. Would Noriko like to come? She asks if the ticket was bought for her. He says yes. Really? Of course. 'I wonder,' she says – though if anything this is the less innocent explanation for an offer she regards as somehow compromising. Hattori assures her that his fiancée wouldn't mind, but Noriko is still uneasy, saying that she'd rather not. She doesn't want to cause trouble.

Hattori's fiancée, like the chemical graduate, makes no appearance in the film, so the viewer has no chance to assess the situation from another point of view, to triangulate the emotional topography however crudely. We're just left with the givens of the scene, Hattori's offer with its possible shadow of impropriety, Noriko's discomfort with its possible element of over-reaction, excessive scruple. This obscurely charged piece of byplay suggests one of two things: either she has difficulty in disentangling the sexual from the merely friendly, or he is deliberately blurring those categories.

The conversation has reached a stalemate. Hattori breaks the tension by saying, 'Are the pickles all stuck together?' 'Yes,' she says, laughing, 'my knife isn't very sharp.' And here we are back to pickle talk, in all its cryptic salinity. (There's one reference to pickles between the two scenes involving Hattori and Noriko – when the professor announces, 'Your aunt gave us some pickles' – but I can do nothing with that, absolutely nothing. Aunt's knife seems sharp enough.)

The jealousy theme supposedly represented by the tell-tale clumping of pickles doesn't begin to add up. Noriko is hardly jealous – she's trying to make sure that she doesn't give offence to Hattori's intended. Mind you, there can be something evasive, even manipulative, about someone who claims to be behaving righteously for the sake of a third party. It seems to leave room for second thoughts. *If things were different . . . (I might give you a better answer).*

Whether her suspicions are exaggerated or justified, her own motives pure or impure, Noriko has ruled herself out as Hattori's concert companion. The next scene shows us the lobby of the concert hall. A woman enters from the left, and for a moment audiences of the film, manipulated by a long history of narrative conventions are bound to think it's Noriko. There are binding contracts of genre from which it isn't easy for any individual film to negotiate an exemption. If there isn't a love theme, however muted, why does Hattori reappear in the action at all? Can all those pickles really only be appetisers for a dish that never arrives? That sounds like a recipe for genre indigestion.

The woman entering the shot is an usherette. She confers inconspicuously with a colleague, and passes on a slip of paper. It's such a quiet moment, coming immediately after the tiny disappointment of realising that Noriko isn't taking advantage of her genre opportunities, that it's easy to miss the implication. What sort of paper slip is it that must be handed here from one usherette to another, as the first one goes off shift, and requires a few words of explanation to pass between them also? A ticket, that's what, a ticket for the concert already well under way, whose purchaser is in the auditorium. The spare ticket is no use inside the concert hall. Its fading validity only has meaning in the public space outside, where someone might come to pick it up.

The message that needs to be passed on isn't hard to work out: the lady is to be admitted however late she arrives. The music isn't the point, after all, and despite Noriko's firm refusal Hattori hasn't given up his hopes, even if he's practical enough to use the vacant seat next to him as a parking place for his briefcase and hat.

Teasing out latent detail in this way is permissible, I take it, as long as you don't have religious objections to an Ozu film being treated as a realist text. Let's say, rather, a part-time realist text. Part-time realism is a description which would also fit, oh, *Madame Bovary*, *Ulysses*, *A la recherche . . .* and as those cases tend to show, it's as much of a mistake to short-change the element of realism as to assume it's all that there is.

Immediately after making clear that Hattori is waiting in vain, Ozu shows us Noriko walking along a city street, a shot which both confirms the previous scene (she never showed up) and calls it subtly into question – why show her to us in the act of staying away, if the decision was really as clear-cut as she made out in the coffee shop?

The distinctive quality of Ozu's cinema is made up of these little contradicting ripples of narrative and feeling. He intensifies the effect when he does something that he's famous for 'never' doing, such as moving the camera. He moves it now. It follows Noriko on her way down the street, though it's placed at the usual low angle. Her body language keeps its secrets. Then Ozu cuts to show her from the front, though her face is not expressive. The camera is still moving! It's a little higher in this second shot, as if what it was undertaking was a timid experiment in hemlines. It was definitely below the knee a moment ago, but now it creeps slightly above knee level. The next shot shows a tree on the pavement, and the camera stays put watching it, like a convalescent needing time to recover, breathless after the unaccustomed exertion, as Noriko walks by. By rights this should be a sequence of turbulent emotion, with the sudden shift of film language putting everything in italics, but Senji Ito's music won't permit that. It's vacuously serene, and the mood it imposes is definite enough, in the absence of strong signals from Noriko's face, to neutralise any suggestion of turmoil.

In contemporary films, American ones above all, cues of music function as sticky strips of prefabricated mood to hold the anonymous artefact together, telling us exactly what to feel though there's rarely any doubt, reinforcing synthetic emotions which despite their exaggerated expression (or because of it) don't actually engage with feeling. The music in *Late Spring* works rather differently, and though I don't happen to like it (the main recurring cue for the film sounds to me like a smeary rendition of 'Amazing Grace') I welcome the way it is used as something more than a honey glaze for images.

The emptily serene music continues into the next

shot, which shows the professor at home waiting for Noriko to return. He hardly looks up when he hears the bells on the sliding door. The music slows down, as if to convey in audible terms the tiredness that goes with arriving home at last.

If the professor is expecting Noriko (and who else could it be?) then the same goes double for the audience. In fact it's the first appearance, after more than half an hour of screen time, of Aya the divorcée, an old school friend of Noriko's. Her entry can only be a surprise, since she hasn't so much as been mentioned before, though she has a major part to play in what follows.

I've read criticism of *Late Spring* which makes out that Aya is intended as some sort of dreadful warning of the fate that awaits Noriko if she doesn't marry, but you have to screen out an awful lot of the film as it develops to sustain that reading of the character.

Aya makes clear in her chat with the professor that she's employed, not as a mere typist but a stenographer. She earns good money. She's not in a hurry to remarry, though she doesn't rule it out even when encouraged to by Professor Somiya. True, she dislikes her ex-husband and hopes not to meet him again. She is rather petulant on the subject, but the professor is entertained rather than disapproving. If Aya is a bad example for his daughter, even a bad influence, then he seems not to have noticed. He asks what her parents think of her marital escapade, but is sympathetic to her rather than to them.

The professor seems very much at ease with her – while he talks he strokes the sides of his nose with a mysterious dark cylinder like a wand of polished black chalk. What is it exactly? I've no idea. I was hoping you'd tell me. A Zen cure for blackheads?

In fact it seems to be the cigarette holder we see him using at various points in the film, though stroking his nose with it while chatting with his daughter's divorced friend seems rather eccentric.

He performed the same odd trick during his first scene with his sister Masa [at 25:25], dislodging the cigarette butt from the holder before stroking both sides of his nose with it. The holder must still be warm, which adds a little extra oddity to the mannerism. At all events, a perverse piece of behaviour to display in front of anyone you don't know well. Perhaps Aya counts as family.

Aya exemplifies the film's postural theme in an extreme form. After a few minutes in the traditional position on the floor her legs have gone to sleep. Acquiescence is no longer a physical possibility for her. It's self-assertion all the way in future, from the modest throne of a Western-style chair.

Western audiences of Ozu's *Tokyo Story*, particularly those over a certain age, tend to exclaim over the enviable suppleness of the old couple in the film (though the actor playing the father is younger than the part he plays – it's Chishu Ryu, the professor here in *Late Spring*). They are able to take up and maintain the traditional position on the floor without effort or strain. Since *Tokyo Story* is among other things about the slackening of traditional family ties, though, it's not clear that the doormat posture has served them well. Perhaps if they installed themselves firmly in Western chairs they would be rewarded with something better than the benign neglect of their children.

When Noriko comes home, she and Aya retreat to Noriko's room upstairs, which is furnished in the Western style. Aya, fresh from a school reunion, has plenty of flighty gossip to pass on, and some of her animation seems to rub off on Noriko.

Their conversation is just a little racier than Westerners would expect to come from well-brought-up Japanese women in 1949. Perhaps sitting in armchairs promotes frankness, just as the *tatami* mat enforces reticence. They talk about one schoolmate who is seven months pregnant, and unmarried.

In the middle of this discussion comes a witty and disorienting moment. The women suddenly stand up, lean towards each other across the table and exchange whispers behind cupped hands. What indiscretion they are sharing graver than unmarried motherhood is impossible to guess. Noriko seems mildly scandalised, saying 'How horrible,' but Aya is worldly enough to say, 'These things happen. Divine Providence, you know.'

The exchange of whispers is a stylised moment that paradoxically points up the artificiality of what has gone before, two young women sharing their most disrespectful thoughts in the company of a film camera and, therefore, thousands of strangers. Viewers of *Late Spring* may feel a twinge of voyeurism at the idea, though the gesture of cupping hands and whispering doesn't necessarily mean that the characters have become post-modernistically aware of this unseen audience. There are plenty of people who lower their voices and mime looking around, even in private, to act out the importance of a secret about to be revealed. Whatever else it does, this whispered confidence of an indeterminately horrible nature makes clear that even in this free-and-easy atmosphere, there is a limit to what can be passed on directly.

The encounter with her old friend (old though new to us) shows a new side to Noriko. The two young women hold hands in the professor's presence and swing their arms [37:54] with a coltish impatience to be girls together. When they reach the stairs, Noriko gives Aya a playful push to help her on her way up to her room.

The idea that Noriko is some sort of prude is quietly refuted in this sequence. She's less worldly than Aya, but that's hardly surprising considering the divergence of their experience, and she takes real pleasure (up to a point) in Aya's dishing the dirt about mutual friends. She'd certainly rather talk scandal than respectable life choices, when Aya presses her to get married. 'Look who's talking,' says Noriko. 'You don't have the right to say that.'

'I do, with authority.'

'No you don't. You're a divorcée.'

In fact Aya regards herself as still being in the game and can't understand why Noriko is so unwilling to play. The little deadlock between them is only broken when they agree to eat something. Noriko asks Aya if she wants some jam on her bread. She asks for 'just a little bit', which Noriko correctly interprets as meaning a lot. When she goes downstairs to fetch it, there's another hint of midnight-feast childishness in Noriko, a definite feel of stockinged-feet stealth about her movements, more tiptoeing caution than would be required simply to avoid disturbing her father's sleep.

The little surge of energy provided by a new character contrasting with the heroine, and complementing her in such surprising ways, masks a small but significant development of implied narrative. Aya's first question to Noriko when they're alone is 'Why didn't you come to the reunion?' Noriko distracts her by asking who was there, but the answer isn't hard to work out. She didn't go to the reunion because she was busy. She was busy not going to the cello recital with Hattori.

When she returned home at last her father asked her if she needed dinner, and she said no, she had already eaten. Only a minute or two later she admits to Aya that she's 'starving'. These hints, taken together, strongly suggest that the travelling shots of Noriko walking through darkened city streets, with their heightened film language, represent a lot of preoccupied wandering, hours of indecisiveness.

Misdirection again. Surprise at the unannounced, unprefigured arrival of Aya and uncertainty about her place in the story prevents us from making sense of the hints given by the previous sequence. It turns out later that Aya lives in Tokyo, which is about 30 miles from Kamakura. Presumably she calls in on the professor's house on her way home from the reunion, perhaps hoping for a bed for the night, and to see what has happened to Noriko – who has been in Tokyo all evening, being indecisive about Hattori.

I don't know what proportion of the audiences watching *Late Spring* over the years has noticed these elements of latent drama. A tiny one. We're so used to important moments being accompanied by fanfares and drum rolls, picked out with spotlights, that oblique statements can simply fail to register. The proportion noticing would presumably have been higher if Ozu had used music less inanely, oppressively placid, perhaps even no music at all, to accompany the images of his heroine's troubled wanderings.

Everything about the Hattori not-exactly-love theme has been squashed and foreshortened, its rhythms broken, tone uncertain, so you could

74

certainly say that this inconclusive ending, this trailing away of possibility, is in keeping. As a plot-strand it has an odd intermediate status, neither open nor closed. Lack of essence seems to be its essential characteristic.

This hasn't been so much a path as a nest of false trails, strewn with pickles and inappropriate music. And perhaps there are other things in the film, equally important, that live a similar half-life, not buried but waiting – murmurs that require active listening, rather than secrets needing to be heroically excavated from hiding-places in the film. Not messages in invisible ink but lucid messages tucked inconspicuously away.

I present the last gasp of the Hattori strand here, out of sequence, because it draws so little attention on first viewing, but though it follows soon after the beach scene its implications are very different. It becomes increasingly strange the more often you see the film. If there's one thing we know (or think we know) about Noriko it's that she has no desire to leave her father's household. Any sort of entanglement with Hattori would complicate things almost more than getting married, with none of the likely benefits. This can hardly be a case of the lure of forbidden fruit, since she has seemed to have so little taste for fruit of any description.

It's hard to see what his attraction could be in this context, though of course she does know him (not a small thing in hierarchical societies, with their limited opportunities for free association) and she feels at ease with him. When her father, after the expedition to the beach, asked if Hattori would make a good husband, she had answered, 'I'm sure he would.'

'Would he?'

'He's very gentle.'

There must be other gentle men in Japan, all the same. Why would she assume there's a shortage?

The late-arriving hint that Noriko has some interest in Hattori sends the veteran, the nuance-hardened viewer of *Late Spring* back to the earlier scene, the one in which she teased her father for his ignorance of this suitable man's unsuitability. Is there something a little off about the acting? Are there some odd false notes?

It's not exactly outrageous to describe the acting style of *Late Spring* as naturalistic, though hard to defend the proposition philosophically – if different cultures had the same idea about what constitutes natural behaviour, how would they differ as cultures? We have to rely on the assistance of common sense, so keen to help, so suspect in its judgements. Is it natural, for instance, to equate spitting in a stranger's face with rudeness? No, since it's possible to imagine a culture where it's a sign of respect. But you'd want to be very sure of your ground before you tried it out on holiday.

76

Even the character of Aunt Masa, the closest to a caricature in the film, isn't particularly stylised, in the playing of Haruko Sugimura. Her avid meddling is anything but attractive, and her idea of a good-luck mascot would be most's people's idea of stolen goods, but she seems sincere when she says that she 'needs to know' how Noriko feels about the possibility of her father marrying Mrs Miwa, that 'sound woman with good taste'. This consideration for her niece's emotions (irrelevant, surely, by any traditional standard) is the closest she comes to a modern moment, and Noriko misses it. She's too upset to notice a kindness that is out of character – unless she sees through it, and recognises it as being no more than the victor's show of mercy to the losing side.

Yet in the scene which leads up to the little revelation of Hattori's engagement, the acting of Chishu Ryu is uncharacteristically broad, even clownish. When he thinks that his assistant and his daughter might make a match of it he grins and struts around the room, and when he learns that his hopes are misplaced he can't seem to take it in.

Setsuko Hara overplays Noriko's emotions in the scene to at least the same degree. After the discussion of Hattori's merits as a husband for someone, and Noriko saying 'I like his type', it's not exactly hard to follow the professor's thought processes when he starts a sentence with 'Your aunt was wondering . . .'

'About what?' Hara opens her eyes exaggeratedly

wide, seeming to signal a refusal to follow rather than actual puzzlement. Then when her father comes out with 'About you . . . marrying him', she laughs so hard she chokes. She has to ask for some tea to help her recover. Perhaps there's some hysteria in this reaction, though without the ambiguities around the cello concert there would hardly be an objection to taking it at face value.

Still, there it is. Does she want a very gentle man or no man at all? At times she seems to have trouble making up her mind.

I keep on saying 'cello concert', although the fuller subtitles of the BFI version of the film, translating the poster, make it clear that the instrument is actually a violin. The name of the soloist even comes into the dialogue in this version ('Noriko, Mari Iwamoto's playing in concert. Want to come?'). In the passage of music we hear, the violin stays in the low end of its register. Perhaps it's just that the cello seems closer to being Noriko's likely representative among the instruments of the orchestra.

In the spectrum of adherence to tradition in *Late Spring*, with Aunt Masa in the ultra-violet range, Aya would be infra-red. Yet she's very matter-of-factly characterised. You would never know from the film how recent, and how alien, was the category of the divorced woman at the time it was made. In an American film like *The Women*, George Cukor's 1939 film version of Clare Boothe Luce's play, divorce is almost a rite of passage, part of becoming adult. Individual reactions to marital break-up may range from stoicism through bitterness to hysteria, but there is a definite sense of shared experience. There's quite a party on the train to Nevada (where the women need to establish residence in order to be free in the shortest possible time). There are long-laid tracks for the divorce express to travel on, and the humour too has a healing sting of familiarity. They're off to Reno, Nevada to be Reno-vated.

Aya's new life is much more of a pioneer venture. If getting divorced for the characters in *The Women* is just another way of being American, then the same is true for her. It's another way of being American. Aya, played by Yumeji Tsukioka, is comprehensively Westernised. Every aspect of her life, from dress, diet and decor to family status and occupation is one long, almost meticulous repudiation of her cultural identity. Her job as a stenographer, taking English shorthand (as she explains to the professor with some pride), means that she works for the dominant, swarming, invisible forces of occupation, who drink the Coca-Cola that nobody serves and nobody sees.

Her public existence is Westernised, and the same goes for her private life. Divorce became legal in Japan only the year before *Late Spring*, on the 1st of January 1948, as part of a package of liberalising measures pushed through the democratic machinery, itself recently installed or imposed. *Late Spring* shows a rapidity of response to changes in society that is journalistic, if not positively tabloid. Aya is not only driving her own train, she's laying her own tracks.

If Ozu and his co-writer Kogo Noda had wanted to treat divorce sympathetically as a social issue, as a solution rather than a problem, the obvious thing to do would have been to tell the story of an unhappy wife, bullied, perhaps even physically abused, who is able to escape her misery at last thanks to some enlightened legislation. (They seem to have had very little interest, generally, in the obvious thing.) By choosing instead an extreme case of the divorced woman, someone just about as Westernised as it is possible to be, they risk taking the character over into the territory of satire, but that isn't how it works in practice.

Extensive contact with Americans has made Aya an adept of instant communication without half-tones. The life of her face comes far closer to the surface, compared with the other characters we see. In her conversation with the professor she is flirty, charming, demanding. In the scene upstairs with Noriko she presents a fascinating contrast with her old schoolfriend. Her immediacy of response and relative lack of mystery mean that she seems if anything the younger of the two, despite her greater experience of life. Her hunger for endorsement is much the greater.

Aya's ex-husband is called Ken, immediately glossed by the professor as Kenkichi, but perhaps for a moment we're supposed to think that she has even married out of her culture. By rights she should be a pariah in the film, a dreadful warning indeed, but she's likeable and seems not to have forfeited anything by her comprehensive loosening of ties with Japanese culture (though it's true that no social collision is engineered between her and Aunt Masa). At an important moment, late in the film, she addresses the professor with a combination of emotional and moral authority, offering sympathy but also a hint of criticism.

The package of measures that included the introduction of divorce also established that citizens over the age of twenty could get married without their parents' permission. Whatever other functions the character of Aya performs in the film, she is a living reminder that everyone is now living in a society where parents can neither dictate the terms of a marriage nor prevent one from happening.

The scene between Noriko and her aunt at Masa's house is the most richly dramatic encounter in *Late Spring*. Both parties seem to agree on what is involved, and on its importance, something which isn't the case for much of the rest of the film. From this point on, Noriko and her father spend a lot of time emotionally at cross purposes.

One of the most basic formulas of melodrama,

if not the most basic, is the escalation of conflict. A chance remark or a small misunderstanding leads to slowly simmering tension, and the discharge of feelings long banked down.

That's not necessarily how it works in *Late Spring*. Noriko has received a great blow from her aunt, with the news that her father is thinking of remarriage. What we see in her next scene with him is her (in modern parlance) 'acting out', advertising her grievances, while he pays no attention whatever. It isn't even that he bites back his annoyance – he shows no signs of noticing the change in the closest person in his life, someone he deals with intimately every day.

Foreign audiences of films, particularly films set in an exotic culture, are understandably tentative about interpreting the behaviour on offer. When in doubt, we wait for a reaction shot or an explicit comment for a clear indication. I don't know how a Japanese audience would read these passages of the film, either at the time of the film's release or now, but it may be that the professor's lack of reaction leads Western audiences to assume that Noriko remains within the norm of acceptable daughterly conduct.

Not likely. This can hardly be so.

When she comes home after Masa's unwelcome revelations, Noriko shuts her father out very firmly. He asks a neutral question ('How was it at your aunt's?') which she evades – 'Nothing special' – though she looks stricken. She ignores his offer of a bath and goes to her room. Her lack of response leads him to follow her upstairs.

We're at a very early stage here in the evolution of intergenerational conflict, virtually the stone age. It will take many thousand baffled man-years before fathers learn even so rudimentary a manœuvre as shouting upstairs, 'Stop this nonsense and come down this minute, young lady! While you live in my house you play by my rules!' Meekly the professor yields the initiative and follows her upstairs to her room.

She's sitting in a chair, from which she looks at him coldly. He keeps asking her what's wrong. She says nothing. Then she gets to her feet and hurries past him out of the room, with her head turned away. He follows her, thoroughly baffled, until it becomes clear that she's leaving the house again. She picks up her bag, still without a word or a glance in his direction. 'Where are you going?' he asks her.

She stops on the way out. She has to. The reason is that same difference between Japanese and American living habits which Ozu pointed out a decade and a half before he made *Late Spring*. She has to stop and put on her shoes. A Western woman could sweep out and slam the door behind her in a single fluent emotional moment, a practised flounce, but Noriko must pause and make adjustments to her costume on the threshold of the home she is rejecting. Centuries of politeness have pooled here and can't simply be stepped over without acknowledgement. She speaks to her father at last, though she keeps her face turned away from him, to say she is going shopping. It's an obvious untruth but not an actual insult. Her rudeness remains passive and doesn't burst out in angry reproaches.

For Noriko to avoid her father's eyes on the way out of her room is a much easier matter than it was when she was trying to slip out from under the hypnotic control of her matchmaker aunt. In her own Western-style chair she's already halfway to standing, and once she's upright she only needs to keep her head turned away while she walks. The earlier avoidance of eye contact was somehow heroic, but this one is not. Noriko is punishing an innocent rather than struggling for survival.

It's true that her father's innocence, the fact that he has no wish to marry again, only becomes clear at the end of the film. I can't honestly remember that first viewing, and how strongly I believed that the professor was following his own desires, rather than conspiring unwisely against his own happiness and perhaps his daughter's. In this scene it's hard not to see his vulnerability. There he is, sitting comfortably on the mat after his bath, cutting his toenails, when there comes in a woman only superficially like the daughter we have seen before, cold and somehow accusatory. She doesn't answer his questions, so he follows her upstairs, but then she walks past as if she couldn't bear to be close to him. She sweeps out of the house with a transparent excuse. And how has he betrayed her, what has his crime been? To tell her the bath is at just the temperature she likes it – brute that he is. (Westerners may need reminding that in Japan the business of cleaning onself precedes the bath. There would be nothing creepy, unhygienic or implicitly incestuous about Noriko luxuriating in the bathwater her father had used.)

Conventional scene construction would end with a shot of the professor's face, to underline his be-wilderment, but that would also provide an artificial tidying away of Noriko's emotions, whose startling turbulence is the most striking aspect of the scene. In-stead the camera shows us Noriko leaving the house and hurrying away, though her pace soon slows. On the soundtrack plays that infernal 'Amazing Grace' cue, but at least it's in the minor for once.

In the short term Noriko's behaviour doesn't improve, but there never comes a moment when her father talks to someone (his sister Masa, Hattori, or even Aya) and says, 'I don't know what's eating that lovely girl of mine. She used to be so full of fun.' Nor does he speak to her directly, saying: 'You'd better think twice about trying this sort of routine when you're married. Your dear old Dad will put up with it, but no husband in his right mind will be so long-suffering.' In melodrama the character's feelings are always being dammed and channelled, funnelled to the moment when all the banks burst and someone cries out, 'Don't you see I've always loved you?' (Or 'hated you' – either will serve its turn.) Here something different happens. Noriko's feelings are allowed to flood out over the whole alluvial plain of her previous happiness.

It isn't melodramatic for the professor to make no protest, and it isn't exactly realistic either. At this point the film has clocked off in terms of realism and is moonlighting in some other mode nearby. The world of *Late Spring* never stops being a recognisable world in which it makes sense to cut your toenails over a piece of newspaper while they're still soft from the bath, but certain rules are relaxed.

This piece of (un)dramatic construction means we see an extreme emotional state acted out without its being contested or explained. It makes an oddly muted impact, seeming to hang there without an echo. If melodrama claps its characters briskly together, then this is the sound of one hand clapping, and perhaps Ozu really was some sort of Zen master after all.

There's a little film criticism (a very little, actually) which addresses Ozu's women and even the possibility of their entertaining darker emotions – notably 'Ozu's Angry Women' by Shigehiko Hasumi, dating from 2003 and written for an Ozu centenary conference at Columbia. Even so it seems remarkably timid, concentrating on 'gestures of indignation' in

Ozu's films. Hasumi looks at three post-'Noriko trilogy' films (*Tokyo Twilight*, *The End of the Summer* and *An Autumn Afternoon*) and offers no extended analysis of *Late Spring*, though he does understandably express surprise that David Bordwell should privilege the father's emotions over the daughter's by classifying it as a 'parent-film'. (Forgivably or not, I assumed that Shigehiko Hasumi was a woman, and had to change the pronouns around after a little research had taught me to know better.)

Hasumi's focus is narrow. He concentrates on moments that combine strong emotion and textiles:

we find many cases of women, both married and single, performing gestures of anger. They show their emotional reaction not by raising their voices or changing their expressions – only with their bodily actions. And what is required for those gestures is no more than an ordinary piece of cloth – a towel or a neckerchief. Whenever I see one of these props in the hands of a young Ozu woman, I grow tense with the expectation that the screen will soon reverberate with her anger.

I admit that I'm not especially sensitive to the misadventures of cloth, in an Ozu film or anywhere else, and to my mind Hasumi refers to the various fabrics almost in the manner of the sexual obsessive, who smuggles the material of his fetishistic obsession (be it latex or chintz) into the discussion for the sheer excitement of seeing the magic words on the page, feeling their potency on his lips:

The tragedy of *An Autumn Afternoon* is that the father is not perceptive enough to recognise his daughter's anger as expressed by her gesture of tossing away the towel.

That action of pulling the towel or neckerchief away from the neck is very brief and might even be missed, but as such it plays an important role in enlivening the scene. In this visual expression of distrust, conveyed not emotionally through words or facial expressions but with an instantaneous, deadpan motion, I see the modernism of Ozu's *mise en scène*.

It is true that almost all of the characters seem to accept the course of events without resistance, and refrain from stirring up the story. But does that mean that the scenes of women yanking towels or neckerchiefs from their necks or suddenly throwing down armfuls of clothing are merely peripheral episodes?

No textiles play a part in the scene of Noriko rejecting the bath prepared for her, but surely the intensity of her distress still registers.

Is it too much to compare Setsuko Hara in this scene, looking with new eyes at the home which had seemed to protect her so well, treating her father as if he was a ghost she was determined not to see, with Jessica Tandy as the mother in Hitchcock's *The Birds*, stumbling past even her beloved son after she finds the pecked body in the farmhouse? Of course it is, but there's a surprising almost-overlap between the two scenes just the same – a sense of all human connection being severed, after a great shock.

In Shigehiko Hasumi's analysis of Ozu, those brief moments of yanking, pulling, tossing and throwing down counterpoint the docile picking up of clothes which is part of the women's daily life and duty. A man comes home from work (as the professor does in *Late Spring*), wearing Western costume, and changes into a *kimono*. A woman follows him, gathering up the clothes he has scattered around the room and putting them neatly away. This looks like the old trope of men not being able to pick up after themselves, though it would be worth finding out if the same cavalier treatment is ever given to traditional clothing. Perhaps the men are doing a little culturally laden cloth-tossing of their own.

It's true that Noriko performs this faintly demeaning chore, but she herself benefits from any number of little attentions. There's that bath that she ignores, despite its ideal temperature. And on the evening of the two missed dates, reunion and cello concert, her father asked whether she'd eaten, when she came in – not in the tones of *Where's my dinner?*, more of *Can I get you something?*

The character of the household, as we have seen it to date, has been set by softly interlocking routines. Father and daughter pad in and out of shot on the little agreed errands between rooms which weave together that other, impalpable textile, a life lived in company. Father and daughter remain on speaking terms, they even go on a sort of farewell tour together to visit Kyoto, but we don't see that household again, its loving rhythms and psychological vitality.

We don't know what happens after Noriko leaves the house to do her 'shopping'. There's a lapse of time between that sequence and the next one. Impossible to say how long. There's one of those scenic sorbets, a 'pillow shot' to cleanse the palate of the mind, bridging the gap, this one showing a wooded hillside. The music is cheerfully pastoral – is it significant that of the four trees visible on the crest of the hill, only one has leaves? One has been stripped even of its branches. The war, after all, has not been over for long.

In fact the same pillow shot (not really a standard term in Japanese aesthetics) was used much earlier, after the opening scene of the tea ceremony, but a pillow can be changed by its emotional context (can't it?), by a sleepless night or an episode of tears, while remaining the same pillow from a strict haberdashery point of view.

There's a possibility that transitional sequences of this type have something to do with the studio as well as the director. After the Great Kanto Earthquake of 1923, Shochiku Kamata was the only major studio left in Tokyo. It made sense to capitalise on this advantage over its rivals by including scenes of the city in the films it made. But even if there is an element of house style involved, Ozu uses the device very personally, both in self-contained transition sequences, like the hilltop with its trees, and in 'pillow shots' within a sequence, Kristin Thompson prefers to call these 'non-POV cutaways' (POV standing for point of view), and says, in a telling phrase, that they 'wedge apart the smooth flow of narrative action'.

After the trees on the hilltop the camera returns us to the professor's house. The handyman is busy outside in the garden [50:17], and the housekeeper is doing some mending. There's someone at the door. She goes to greet him. The visitor is Hattori.

Hold on a minute. Handyman. Housekeeper. What handyman? What housekeeper? We've never seen these people before. Can we be sure this is even the same house?

Hattori, at least, seems to take it all in his stride. He has brought something in a box, a thank-you present, along with a large envelope. The housekeeper explains that the professor and Noriko have gone to the performance of a Noh play.

When Hattori has gone the housekeeper opens the envelope and takes a good look at the wedding portrait it contains ('Isn't it an amazing photo? It looks just like him. Such a beautiful bride!'). She also mentions to the handyman that she thought Hattori was going to marry Noriko. He thought so too. Then he tells her he's going to chop some wood.

Who are these people?

An explanation that might make sense would be: Noriko has agreed to marry in the unspecified interval since the last scene, and consequently the household has been supplemented to prepare for her departure to her new life.

This possibility is knocked on the head by the remark about her being expected to marry Hattori, not something a newcomer could know. This whole scene with the domestic staff is the narrative equivalent of an impossible object, at odds with the laws of perspective.

Violation of sequence along these lines became more or less a standard feature in European art films of the 1950s and 60s. Resnais might use such a device to challenge the tyranny of memory, Bunuel to tease the bourgeois mania for tidy stories. Insert it in a Japanese film from 1949 and nobody pays the blindest bit of notice. Perhaps it's considered bad manners to point out the joke-shop balsa boulder in the Zen gravel garden.

These people, housekeeper and handyman, are here on the professor's premises right now, they seem to feel at home (the housekeeper hardly looks up when the bells on the door announce someone coming in), they refer to past incidents, and so audiences accept that they must always have been there. Never mind the thousand domestic details in the film to date that are entirely dependent on father and daughter constituting the entire population of the house: Noriko warming the *sake* for her father and Onodera, though she succeeds only in making it lukewarm (she promises to do better with the next flask). The professor preparing his own bath and telling Noriko it's just at the right temperature for her. Hattori having to help the electrician with a stool in this unambiguously unstaffed establishment.

Clearly realism hasn't clocked on again just yet. It's a disorienting little scene altogether, with these retainers apparently grown at short notice like a crop of cress on damp blotting-paper, mysteriously privy to family history.

Whatever the existential status of the newcomers, they make clear that this is no longer a household where domestic tasks are undertaken with fluid familiarity by people who are constant presences in each other's minds. If the household is now staffed it means that in the future things will be done by hired help. For the bath to reach an ideal temperature will be a matter of high professional standards rather than tender thoughtfulness.

When we first see her, the housekeeper is busy with her needle and thread, which clashes faintly but distinctly with the opening scene, where Aunt Masa recruited Noriko to do her mending for her. There was no suggestion then that Noriko had the option of delegating.

Misdirection is a technique Ozu has used before in the film, and even in this specific form, the introduction of new characters. If Aya was presented in such a way as to draw some of our attention away from Noriko's tiny crisis over Hattori, then what are we being distracted from here? It's hard to be sure – perhaps to mask the discontinuity between the Noriko we saw last, leaving her house in disarray, and the highly composed personage we see at the start of the next scene. That would be a good joke, to mask the emotional discontinuity in your leading lady by way of a far grosser discontinuity: household members abruptly emerging from the drawer in which they've lived till now and taking up their duties of gardening and darning.

It's like the moment in a science-fiction film where feckless use of the time machine has changed the past, and travellers return to a world that has been fundamentally (or trivially) altered. Except that audiences of the film seem to have gone along on the metaphysical ride too, so that they have been altered themselves, and entirely fail to spot the transformation in circumstances.

We do love our continuity.

The scene with the servants from a parallel universe breaks the formal flow of the film, but also prepares for the next one, at the Noh drama announced by the housekeeper. If the vase in the Kyoto inn is the most famous image in *Late Spring*, then this is the most famous scene. It's not straightforward, just the same. For one thing, the scene is long, and audiences will need to engage with what's on stage as well as off (to wit, Noriko's change of mood) for that length to be justified. I find it hard going.

Fond Occidentalising fantasy proposes that a person such as Noriko, set down on an English seaside pier in front of a striped booth to watch a performance of Punch and Judy (let's say a run-through, so she can't be cued by audience reaction) would readily identify the mode of the show as comedy, the tone harsh, its subject-matter the horror of marriage, stupidity of policemen, fragility of babies, slyness of crocodiles. We, on the other hand (or simply I), can make no such analytic progress when confronted with the Noh, either in *Late Spring* or anywhere else.

For Western audiences, the classical forms of theatre represent sheer unassimilable Japaneseness. And if I feel estranged from the spectacle in this scene, I have something of the same feeling about the spectators, about Noriko and her father. They sit side by side with an expression of patient composure that suggests a formal family photo. Have they patched it up? How? When? On whose terms? At whose instigation?

The last time we saw Noriko she was being swept out of the house on a flood of turbulent feeling, but here she is, not so much being the professor's daughter as playing that part. This is only the second time we've seen the pair of them out of the house as a unit, and the first was the train ride into Tokyo, which they took together out of convenience and sociability. The emotional contrast between the two expeditions seems very great, as great a difference as exists between dinner eaten in chosen company and a condemned person's last meal. There are no words exchanged between them (not in itself surprising among well-behaved audience members), and there's no eye contact either.

The intervening scene with the servants, its strange incompatibility perhaps subconsciously registering, increases the sense of distance. This Noriko with her withdrawn decorum is as new and incongruous as the housekeeper and handyman. When she was leaving the professor's house in her last scene before this one, she kept her gaze from her father, but now she seems to be withholding herself from us. Because the scene starts with the performance already in progress, we are denied the opportunity of seeing how much father-daughter rapport survives, as we could if we were able to hear them talking before the show,

Consequently the scene, for much of its length, seems to show a rather limited dialogue between extreme styles of Japanese behaviour, the drama on stage so shrill yet unspecific, the human relationship that has become so familiar over the course of the film suddenly chilly and unreadable. Professor Somiya becomes more engrossed in the play (anyone can twinkle their eyes, but somehow Chishu Ryu has the knack of twinkling with his mouth). Noriko doesn't. She remains impassive and preoccupied.

The most obvious way to make sense of the scene is to assume that the Noh play in some way echoes the emotional situation that is being withheld from us. (Even so, there seems to be no point in showing so much of the performance, with the result that subtext displaces text for several minutes.) David Bordwell identifies the play as *Morikawa*, saying it presents 'an explicit parallel in its depiction of an aristocratic woman driven into a frenzy by the memory of a lost lover'. Let's see now – Noriko isn't aristocratic, she's not frenzied, and she has no lost lover to remember. If that's an explicit parallel, I'd hate to meet a shot in the dark.

Internet commentary instead identifies *Kakitsubata* as the drama being performed, in which the soul of an iris attains Buddhahood. I've no idea whether that's right, but at least this idea has some vague transcendence going for it, which could be made to work if absolutely necessary, with the help of a shoehorn – if what we're saying is that Noriko must rise above selfishness and let go of her attachment to her father.

I can see that the scene at the Noh play could have the makings of an overwhelming cinematic sequence, but only if the camera moved. In other words, not in an Ozu film. Max Ophuls was also making great films in the 1940s, and he would have gone to town on this moment – but then he went about things very differently. Theatre was his prevailing metaphor, but it was also the direct opposite of his working method. Whenever his camera moved (and it was rarely still) he delivered an experience that went beyond anything the theatre could match, even when the camera was circling round a theatrical performance.

The Noh scene is uncharacteristic of *Late Spring* because it tells us exactly where we are. The uncertainty principle that has seemed to be the essence of Ozu is currently in abeyance. I know what I'm watching, when the camera fixes on the Noh chorus for very nearly a minute. I just don't know why. Towards the end of the shot the personage to the right of the group, sitting cross-legged in a black costume with a pointy hat, begins to shift around [54.53], but whether preparing to make an entrance or troubled by worms I really couldn't say.

In the Noh sequence there's no attempt to bridge the stark divide between actors and spectators. Is it possible that this is at least part of the point? Instead of the fluid interpenetrating backstage lives we've seen so far, we witness clear separations and formal alignments.

Weak as it is, this line of thinking seems a bit more promising than hoping that identification of the correct Noh play will somehow unlock whatever secrets the sequence might turn out to hold.

There's a little flutter of conventional drama in the scene, rather near its end. This is a seven-minute scene, and well after the four-minute mark the professor puts his right hand on the back of the seat in front of him, and looks over to his left. Noriko looks towards him (though there's still no eye contact) and then in the direction of his glance. We don't see what she sees there, only that she produces a slightly ghastly smile and bow. Finally we see Mrs Miwa returning the courtesy from her seat, with greater elegance and naturalness.

For the next minute or so we watch Noriko's face as it absorbs the new and unwelcome emotional information. Her face seems to curdle, and her eyes slide towards her father, in two stages. Then she looks down again, her mouth working faintly, before looking uncertainly back in the direction of Mrs Miwa.

Next her face sinks almost to the horizontal, in a pose of despair. When she looks back at her father, it is almost with hostility. He doesn't react to her changed demeanour, still radiating his almost-smile of Noh connoisseurship.

She looks over at Mrs Miwa one more time, almost with bitterness, before returning her attention blankly to the stage. Her father's absorption in the stage action means that the only person with whom Noriko has made eye contact in this whole long scene is the very person she fears will evict her from her happiness at home, Mrs Miwa.

We see a comprehensive display of misery,

including resentment, despair and a sense of betrayal, but we don't know exactly what it is all responding to. Is it the simple presence of Mrs Miwa that upsets her, the corroboration of her existence breathing the same air as her father? Is it that Noriko feels the whole expedition was stage-managed, not a gesture towards her but merely part of a programme of getting her accustomed to the presence of her father's future wife? No way of knowing.

As for that aspect of the situation that she doesn't grasp – that her father has no actual intention of remarrying – we are free to think we can detect Aunt Masa's hand (light on a stranger's wallet, heavy on a relative's heart) is at work here in the meeting, or we can assume that Mrs Miwa's presence was accidental. Even so, Professor Somiya presumably understands the impact it will make on Noriko when he acknowledges her.

All we have to go by is Noriko's face. One of the bits of Internet babble about the face of *Late Spring*'s heroine is that it 'seemed like she'd smile even if she were to get hit by a car'. The minute or so of screen time after Noriko has seen Mrs Miwa at the Noh play shows something rather different. The face we see now might never have smiled in its whole life. Noriko hasn't been hit by a car but there's been some sort of collision, undoubtedly, and the smiling mechanism has been badly damaged.

I still find the construction of the scene unsatisfactory. If the camera showed us Mrs Miwa earlier in the sequence then at least there would be some suspense building up before the professor's acknowledgement. Admiring critics describe the Noh scene with the knowledge of what is coming, after seeing it a number of times. There's something wrong with a scene that only begins to work on the second viewing.

The shot which follows on from the Noh sequence makes the whole 'pillow shot' idea seem silly. What we see is a wind-agitated tree against the sky. This isn't a moment of repose but the intensification of an emotional argument, with the tree's agitation standing in for Noriko's mental state. It's the pathetic fallacy in full leaf, nature pressing in to voice and dignify human concerns. The first time I saw that image I think I even gasped. I can't retrieve that feeling now, and I'm not sure how the image, sedate enough out of context, even comforting (the branches aren't exactly thrashing), set it off so strongly then.

Keiko I. McDonald describes the tree as 'leafless', which is clearly wrong, but perhaps points to her having received a similar impression to mine, one of devastation.

Is there anything in terms of film language, the grammar of image and sound, to support the idea that the tree shot, coming at this moment, is somehow a portrait of Noriko's state of mind, rather than a cool image of otherness? Perhaps a little something. The music of the Noh, being performed live on stage, carries over into the tree shot and beyond. This isn't background music but actually part of the previous scene, and inflects the image differently, making it seem emotionally continuous, rather than contrasting.

The next actual scene is of Noriko and her father walking in the street after the Noh, and even here the Noh music persists. In fact there's a sort of soft war on the soundtrack as the blander background score rises through the music of the Noh. This is the only moment in the film to use such a technique of fade in/fade out, and it seems safe to say, considering the technology available in 1949, that the effect took a little work and was strongly intended. Admittedly with Ozu the distinction between the casual and the deliberated is harder to maintain than it is with most film-makers, most artists generally. But this part of the soundtrack was laboured over.

Most of the time Senji Ito's music seems vacuous or actively distracting. The only other part of the soundtrack which shows sign of real care, of being specifically designed to fit the sequence it accompanies, is at the opposite end of Noriko's emotional spectrum, earlier in the film, before the clouds of marriage gather. It's the scene starting at 26:34. She potters around the house on her own doing chores, her body language loose and swinging. She throws some linen onto a chair as if she didn't have a care in the world. Throughout the scene there's a melody on the soundtrack, a song without words. For a moment it even seems possible that this is Noriko singing. Certainly the music is closely matched to her mood. It's a charming domestic vocalise, an emanation of happy housework, though in fact the vibrato is closer to a stringed instrument's or a musical saw. Everything about the soundtrack is carefully managed here, down to the transition to the next scene, where the solo line is plumped out with harmony.

In the scene after the Noh there's another piece of evidence, apart from the care taken over the soundtrack, to bolster the argument that the tree shot is an example of the pathetic fallacy rather than a touch of Zen. It's more intense in itself, but has a lower ontological status, not being part of the finished film. In the original script for *Late Spring* the scene after the Noh was introduced in these terms: *ON THE WAY HOME: A QUIET RESIDENTIAL QUARTER WHICH SUFFERED FROM A WAR DISASTER.* Ozu may have managed, somehow, to retain the sense of blighted domestic life even without the use of such an emotionally explicit setting.

The war between the musics makes its own unsettling contribution to the mood, and even if the blander strain prevails in the end, that isn't how the next scene plays out. Professor Somiya makes post-show small talk, to which Noriko doesn't respond.

'Today's Noh was quite good . . .'

No reply.

'Shall we go to Takigawa to eat? . . .'

No reply.

'What do you think? . . .'

Noriko, who has been walking beside her father, falls behind. He turns towards her in mild surprise. She says 'I have to go somewhere.'

'Where?'

'It's nothing.'

'Will you be late?'

'I don't know.'

She sets off diagonally across the road, swinging her arms, almost at a run [59:53]. Over half a century of youth culture and inter-generational conflict has acquainted us with what's going on. Noriko is having a sulk, a huff, a strop. It's all very teenaged – except that in 1949 the teenager has yet to be invented, even in America, and Japan will not be the first country to import the new product. Not to mention that Noriko is twenty-seven.

In context, her acting-out is extraordinary in its childishness and disarray. For one thing, the place she has chosen for it has very limited topographical possibilities. There's no pavement on the other side of the gravelled road, just an overgrown verge. She makes it very clear that the 'somewhere' she needs to go, to do something which is 'nothing', has a simple definition: anywhere away from her father.

She is actually going in the same direction as he is, which weakens the rhetoric of her breaking away. She doesn't keep up the rapidity of her pace, so that by the end of the sequence they are moving in the same direction at a similar rate, however far apart they are in emotional terms. The professor is still on the pavement and Noriko is in a sort of ambulant exile of her own choosing, on the far side of the gravel road.

If you want to think that the professor has the ghost of a smile on his face as Noriko marches on ahead of him, as if pleased that she's reacted so strongly, there's nothing to stop you. If he does give an infinitesimal smile, then it's already dying at the point when the shot begins, and his face soon reverts to neutrality, so that watching it in real time it's easy to think that nothing happens. The effect is only at all strong if you use the slow-motion function on your DVD player or computer. Peculiar fringe benefit of digital technology! – making possible the scrutiny of a facial expression six decades in the past. The closest thing there is to a time machine.

Professor Somiya smiled to himself more definitely in an earlier scene [it's at 48:38], when he heard Noriko coming in after the wedding project was first broached by Masa, just before she hurried away from the bath, so lovingly drawn, as if it was full of acid. These two underplayed facial expressions are the only evidence in the film that Noriko's father is actively conspiring with Masa, though Masa doesn't know he won't be going through with the second part of the scheme, the part that involves him and Mrs Miwa. Both smiles convey his satisfaction that Noriko has taken the bait. Of course she's taken the bait! She's choking on it.

There's no way of knowing what Noriko had in mind when she said, after the Noh, that she needed to go somewhere to do something (which was more precisely nothing), but the setting of the next scene comes as something of a surprise, to us though clearly not to her. It's a rather stately interior, with a grandfather clock and antique furniture. Noriko, waiting in her stockinged feet, might have been transported to a housemaster's study in a public school – never mind that the view through the windows is of a brick wall mere feet away. Noriko's eyes fill with tears, though her mood has lost its defiance and modulated to a pure state of dejection. Quickly and efficiently she wipes the tears from her eyes as soon as the door opens.

In comes Aya, positively bouncing along, taking off the apron she's wearing. Her animation merrily contradicts the decorum of the room. 'Sorry for keeping you waiting,' she says. 'I've been busy making some cakes. I put in too much vanilla. But they're delicious.'

Oh dear. It's even worse than we feared. Aya has been Westernised to the point of madness. Tragic really. Not only has she been taking lessons in morals from America, specifically on the subject of the disposability of husbands, she's also fallen under the spell of British traditions in decor and baking. 'Let's go to the other room,' she say, and comments on how cold Noriko's hands are.

Then she says, to someone unseen, 'Fumi – bring those cakes to that room.' A rather unidiomatic subtitle, and a curious moment altogether. Fumi joins the list of people in *Late Spring* who are mentioned but not shown, even though Fumi is virtually present already, on the other side of a door.

The servant situation here seems to be the reverse of the system at the professor's house. Here domestic help has an acknowledged existence and even a name, but no visual presence, while at the professor's place staff sprout like mushrooms when there's no one at home.

But why mention a servant if she's not going to appear? I imagine the idea is to undermine Aya's rather abrupt impersonation of a homebody. Why would a career woman turn to baking if she pays someone to look after her household needs? Some do, of course, but the scene makes another kind of sense if we assume that the technical comments ('I put in too much vanilla') and the prop of the apron are intended to substantiate a harmless deception, the laying claim to the labour of another. Fumi does the baking and Aya takes the credit.

Aya, having given Fumi her instructions, tosses her apron into the kitchen. Note to Shigehiko Hasumi: flung cloth can express a woman's carefree modernity as well as desperate tension.

The 'other room' continues the theme of Anglo antiques, but in a lighter key. Here are deep armchairs and chairs that hint at country kitchens. Aya pours tea, without ceremony and from quite a height, into cups that have handles and sit on saucers. She adds a good slosh of milk and two sugars to each.

In gastric terms this is reckless. The chance of both Aya and her guest having the congenital ability to tolerate lactose is statistically unpromising: roughly one in a hundred. There's always a price to be paid for assimilation, and there are always things that can't quite be assimilated.

Aya produces two enormous slabs of cake and starts pressing Noriko to eat one. When she announced this treat she described it as shortcake, using a loan-word that sounds like *shotkaiki*. It isn't just the baked-down, biscuity sort of shortcake but the full summer dessert oozing fruit and cream, layers of rich excess.

Not only is the food un-Japanese, the etiquette of offering it contradicts the simpering abasement of traditional manners. The desired emotional etiquette is expressed by the word *enryo*, and the explanation of it given by Yuri Kageyama in his blog even uses cake as an example. The hostess is expected to slander the quality of the cake, while the guest politely disclaims any appetite. Ideally it should take several exchanges of ritual self-belittlement for cake and hungry mouth to be brought satisfactorily together.

Any system of politeness can misfire, of course, as in the story of the English twins who were so polite in the womb (after you, Cyril, no after you, Cecil) that neither ever got born. The required forms of good behaviour can easily hide people from one another, in terms of what they really want.

Cake is something that Noriko really doesn't want. Aya escalates from pronouncing it delicious (which she does three times in all), to wheedling pressure – 'Just a little piece. I made it. Try some!' – and finally to the jocular threat of force: 'Eat it. I'll make you!'

Noriko leaves abruptly, ignoring a hospitality that is becoming increasingly strident. Aya's last words in the scene are 'I thought you would stay over! Stay overnight!' She more or less runs after her escaping guest. You could see this as desperation on her part, sign of the loneliness that is the necessary consequence of untraditional choices, but it's possible to read it a little differently, if you're as stubbornly sympathetic to Aya as I seem to be. Styles of life with no historical precedent, no hold on tradition, stand in great need of corroboration. Aya's Westernised furniture may be heavier and more substantial than the traditional Japanese variety, but it's existentially flimsy, liable to blow away in any breeze.

It may be, too, that Aya stayed the night with Noriko on the evening of the class reunion and the midnight feast, which would make it reasonable for Aya to want to play host in her turn.

You could say that Aya is being insensitive to her friend's state of mind, or you could say that Noriko is clinging to obsolete expressive conventions. She suppresses distress, as tradition expects of a woman, while Aya is Westernised in this way too. In terms of the Hollywood rules by which Aya plays, it's fine to wipe away your tears while a friend enters the room – just as long as you make sure she sees you do it. Noriko's oblique handling of pain and Aya's detuning from nuance conspire to keep them from any real communication.

It must be obvious that the scene at Aya's flat is a parody of the tea ceremony with which *Late Spring* began. It's as punctilious in its inversions as a Black Mass, a piece of methodical cultural blasphemy, but even so the contrast doesn't work altogether in favour of the original ritual.

Teatime at Aya's is a charade but it's still a social event where information and emotion can be exchanged, even if it doesn't happen to work out that way on this occasion. The threat to Noriko's happiness doesn't come from here. In fact it's strongly associated with traditional settings – including, yes, the tea ceremony near the start of the film. Mrs Miwa attends, and is even introduced to Noriko, but she's not 'Mrs Miwa' yet, with all the danger she represents, just a congenial friend of Aunt Masa. By the time of the Noh, though, she has solidified into a blighting presence. It's from these ceremonies, for all the insistent timelessness of their images and symbols, that the change comes which Noriko sees as disastrous. It isn't modernity which betrays her but traditional culture, with its promise of stasis, time frozen while the clocks tick.

Teatime at Aya's isn't a failed ritual but merely a botched communication, a missed opportunity from both women's point of view. Noriko has what few women have had, historically, in any culture, access to someone with sexual experience but no stake in the system – an ex- and therefore a non-wife. If anyone was in a position to inform her about what marriage involves, it would have to be Aya. Instead Noriko asks about how she would go about getting a job.

Aya finds this an irritating question, since she wouldn't have to work if her marriage had been a success ('if Ken had been a decent man'). Why does Noriko want a job of all things? No reason, says Noriko – prompting Aya to say that if you're going to do something for no reason, then you should get married for no reason.

Aya plays down her own accomplishments, her

value in the marketplace, by saying that if she can be a stenographer anyone can. This is evasive, though the evasion, in someone so keen to say the hardly sayable, is more the film's than the character's. To be a stenographer on Aya's level, to afford her spacious flat, antique furniture and domestic (possibly baking) help, you have to speak English, and you have to work for the forces of occupation.

The opportunity missed by Aya is linked to the question Noriko doesn't ask. Why doesn't Noriko want to marry, why doesn't she even want to ask for information about that complex state from someone uniquely well placed to provide it? Why has she ruled it out so decisively, to the point where she contemplates working to support herself, despite the huge practical and social disadvantages, as a preferable option? Noriko can hardly have had any sexual experience. It's Aya who has that, while Noriko is unmarried and respectable. Any attraction she might have had to Hattori was nipped in the bud, or nipped even earlier, nipped in the bulb.

So Aya doesn't ask the question which might seem natural coming from her: 'Dear friend, what is it about the prospect of marriage which fills you with terror and despair?' That question isn't asked anywhere in *Late Spring*, unless you think that the whole film amounts to a posing of the question, and that perhaps it even suggests an answer.

Instead, the conversation between Noriko and

Aya gets bogged down in wrangles. The wrong questions get asked, the right ones melt away. Disagreements about cake overshadow their exchanges and make them fractious, just as pickle quibbles nibbled away at that idyllic scene with Hattori by the sea.

The gap in narrative time between Noriko leaving the house on a distraught shopping errand and the visit to the Noh was indefinite and indefinable. Now scenes follow each other closely, as the continuity of her clothes (a pale suit with a white collar) makes clear. The Noh performance was a matinee, after which Noriko stalked off to Aya's for tea and cake at the appropriate hour for ordeal by lactose. Now, that same evening, she returns home.

The new scene (starting at 1:04:22) follows the same pattern as the last domestic one (48:30 on), which began with the professor cutting his toenails and Noriko arriving in deep distress after the showdown with her aunt. Now Noriko seems relatively calm, though withdrawn rather than genuinely composed. Her 'I'm home' sounds a little sepulchral. She gives the shortest possible answer to her father's question about where she's been, without making eye contact, and is turning to leave the room when he calls for her attention, saying, 'I got a letter from your aunt. She wants you to visit on Saturday. The day after tomorrow.'

Noriko doesn't look at him or reply, but continues on her way upstairs. Ever since she learned which way the wind was blowing (Aunt Masa, cheeks puffed out, propelling Mrs Miwa towards her happiness on a collision course) she has shunned the ground floor of the house, the place of past sharing, and retreats as soon as she can to her own bedroom, where a father's claims are weakest.

On her way through those downstairs spaces she has picked up a towel. Once in her room, Noriko puts it down roughly on a chair, dumping her bag on the table with a slight rolling motion and an evident lack of respect. Then she picks up the towel again, her body taut. It looks for a moment as if she's going to throw it down.

I can't say that reading Shigehiko Hasumi on the anger of Ozu's women has greatly enriched my experience of the films, but I do have a strong mental picture of Hasumi himself getting stirred up at moments like these, when woven items and strong emotions are in close proximity. Then Noriko overrides her own impulse and takes the towel out of shot, her gestures suggesting that she's going to hang it up. Hasumi can relax, though perhaps he feels disappointed, cheated of the tableau that grips his imagination.

Noriko goes downstairs again. She continues to withhold eye contact from her father. He resumes the conversation about Aunt Masa's plan, the conversation Noriko so much wants not to have. 'Go and meet him,' he says. 'He'll be there as well.'

She's looking for something. Finally she finds it – a little bottle. Perhaps something for the bath? 'Can't I refuse to go?' she asks, and he explains that she can always turn the prospect down once she's met him.

She looks at him as if he's completely missing the point, then turns to leave the room. Her silence and refusal to look at him amount to a powerful rejection.

He calls after her, 'Hey . . .' She only half turns, as if to listen to one more short speech on her way out. 'Noriko, come here.'

This is as close as he gets in the whole film to exercising a father's authority, to set limits in however mild a fashion to a dependent daughter's behaviour, persistently sullen and hostile.

She doesn't defy him, though her concessions are slight. She sits when he tells her to, but still keeps her eyes away from him. He starts a whole series of conversational openings (eight of them), about the niceness of Satake, about the necessity of marrying sometime, about this being the right time, without her responding.

Forgive me. I need to press Pause, even rewind a little. I have a bone to pick with Mr Ozu. Noriko's whole looking-for-a-little-bottle routine is very thin. It's not easy to believe that this little bottle of shampoo or unguent (dermabrasion pesto for all I know) even lives downstairs, impossible to believe that she would re-enter the once-shared now-unbearable space to retrieve it at this juncture.

No overambitious interpretation required here. This isn't an active departure from realism, just a lapse from it. Ozu could more plausibly have the professor go upstairs, but he seems very attached to the father's disavowal of his own authority. Of course the moment passes, and the emotional stakes are sufficiently high that audiences either don't notice or cheerfully disregard the way the heroine has been made to act inconsistently in the interests of the confrontation to come. I emphasise the weak moment because it's so very uncharacteristic. The micro-management of drama (drama that is low-key yet oddly intense) by means of simple props and neutral actions is something which in the normal course of things Ozu does supremely well.

Forget the little bottle. Wind forward again. Now Play. When Noriko does finally speak to her father in this scene, she doesn't engage with any part of the agenda he has so patiently been laying out. She starts, 'But I . . .', and when prompted finishes the sentence as 'I want to be with you.' Professor Somiya doesn't point out that for some time now she has been systematically avoiding and ignoring him. Is she even looking at him now? No she's not.

There follows a sort of deference contest, which takes us rather far away from the direct utterance of 'I want to be with you.' Reflexes of self-suppression can make it easy to lose sight of what anyone actually wants. Ozu changes shot, so that instead of alternating between the two of them he shows the professor facing us, with Noriko in a three-quarter profile.

First the professor says having Noriko stay with him would be the most convenient thing possible, but that he's been selfish for long enough. He must apologise. It's time for her to marry – or else he'll worry.

If Aya had been able to brief Noriko for this conversation, she would have advised against her next gambit, which is 'But if I marry, what are you going to do?' *Enryo*, outmoded *enryo*. The professor inevitably protests his self-reliance, Noriko ridicules it, and side-issues crowd out the main debate. She will pay quite a price for not having her emotional agenda ready, complete with bullet-points, and a strategy properly planned.

A change comes over the conversation. In the process of evoking her father's helplessness Noriko remembers the co-operation that used to uphold the household, and she forgets her anger and despair. She raises her eyes to his face, briefly at first and then with sustained attention, as she tells him that without her his shirts and collars would be dirty, that he'd forget to shave in the morning ('Well, I'll shave in the evening,' he puts in), that his desk would be a mess and he would end up burning the rice for his dinner. By the time she tells him he would be in real trouble without her, her voice has taken on much of its old warmth and things are almost back to normal between them.

It can't last. Her father continues in the same slightly unreal register, but introduces just the prospect that she dreads. 'But . . . what if I release you from these worries? For instance, if someone else would look after me?' He seems not to realise that making sure he's well looked after ('these worries'!) constitutes, for whatever reason, the life she wants for herself. She replies sharply 'Which someone?' and they're back at loggerheads.

She presses him to admit his plans, while comparing him to Onodera, who was labelled 'filthy' for remarrying, though her disgust is no less mysterious for being consistent. Her voice verges on the hysterical as she puts him under pressure. He answers her with a series of tiny nods and grunts of assent. With a grimace she turns and runs from the room.

Upstairs she leans against a wardrobe. Now her father does climb the stairs, but in a spirit of conciliation rather than insistence. Hearing him approach, she prepares herself, sitting in a chair with her back half-turned to him. 'Please stay away, Father,' she says. 'Please go downstairs. Please.'

He seems genuinely shocked, as he stands there, by her disproportionate reactions. He opens and closes his fingers uncertainly. Managing a smile, he says, 'Well, please go the day after tomorrow. We're all so worried about you.'

She keeps her head turned away and says nothing. 'You will go, won't you? For my sake.'

At this stage of his pleading, there is no question of his exercising authority of any sort. He asks her a favour. He would take it as a kindness if she agreed to meet the chemical graduate Aunt Masa thinks a suitable match for her.

On his way out of her room he picks up a hanky from the floor and puts it neatly on the table. In the corridor he picks up something else from out of shot, a towel or teatowel, folds it and puts it on a chair. I suppose it's possible that Ozu is showing the professor as taking on a female role here in his powerlessness and bafflement, except that it's much easier to find the 'feminine' parts of Somiya's character than the 'masculine' ones. The film leans over backwards to indicate that this is not, absolutely not, the story of a woman forced into anything, even if it seems wildly unlikely that a Japanese man of some social status born sometime before 1900 would approximate so closely to the uninvented New Man of Western culture. This is a subtler story, about a woman who can't find an alternative to a course of action that mysteriously seems to fill her with horror.

The professor's two textile moments towards the end of this scene, with the hanky and the towel, seem to me much more like further examples of displacement behaviour, gestures intended to reassure the person making them that nothing is seriously wrong. He looks out of the window and says, 'It'll be sunny again tomorrow,' though the remark is so plainly unrelated to the weather that he might have saved himself the trouble of looking.

In the next shot, we see Noriko's tragic face as her father moves away behind her. She weeps, putting her head in her hands. The camera recedes from her in stages, at a slower rate than her father does. Next we see her from behind, still crying. Finally the camera shows us the impassive corridor, in what might qualify as a 'pillow shot' if the sound of her crying didn't carry over into it, compromising any effect of calm.

Whatever patching up there was between father and daughter between Noriko's abrupt shopping trip and the outing to the Noh, it has all unravelled now. Her composure has been stripped from her all over again, and this time there is nowhere for her to go.

Do you remember the servants? The retainers, indoor and outdoor, the housekeeper and the handyman? They've gone again. No sign of them. They've disappeared, and left no trace behind. If you do remember them, you're a freak of nature or an impossible object in your own right – because nobody else does.

If the servants did exist, they would have the most eccentric job description in the history of domestic service, under orders to keep well out of sight when there's anyone in the house, but to pop in when the coast is clear to do a little light tidying of the garden, a little light needlework.

I remember being told in the 1980s that people on different physical levels (on a balcony, say) were socially invisible according to the conventions of Japanese culture. I thought this was a fascinating idea, and a cunning way of multiplying space by changing the definition of privacy – though I did wonder how a split-level flat would work in practice. Was there a minimum size of step below which the sightlines were clear? I have no idea whether this information was true. I certainly have a gullible side, but any doubts I had didn't stop me from passing it on many hundreds of times.

Perhaps this is what is happening with the servants in *Late Spring*? Perhaps as a matter of film convention they don't enter the visual field, being promoted to visibility only when there's no one in the house and they have to deputise for the absentees (as in the scene where Hattori delivers his thank-you present and wedding photograph).

Not really a workable theory, is it? Not when we've just had a long conversation between father and daughter about whether or not he'll be able to manage on his own, in terms of grooming, cooking, laundry and general self-maintenance. It seems to be accepted between them that if she wasn't there to look after him, he would have no one. That's the rationale, after all, for his suggesting getting married himself. If Noriko doesn't have the sense to point out that there are retainers on hand to meet the professor's needs (retainers with the knack of evading human vision, like a cross between Jeeves and the creature in *Predator*), perhaps she doesn't deserve to get what she wants.

In the next scene the professor and Masa pay a visit to a shrine, to enlist supernatural help for a happy outcome to their plans for Noriko. The tone lightens as it goes along, modulating into outright comedy when Masa spots the purse on the ground. She positively scampers to pick it up, an action made ridiculous by her traditional costume, ill-designed for the furtive pounce. She opens the purse and looks inside, though we don't learn what she finds there. Absurdly invigorated by this sign of good luck, or by the windfall it contains, she trots towards a group of pigeons to startle them (another mismatch of costume and conduct) and sets off up a tall stairway at quite a pace and in evident high spirits.

And why not? The professor and his sister are promoting a marriage, and marriage epitomises comedy. Comedy is the genre, pretty much by definition, which ends with a marriage (sometimes more than one). Marriage is a beginning not an end. The match, presented to the bride with a latitude which is greatly in excess of what traditional culture requires, represents the fulfilment of a personal project for Masa, her bit of tidying house. She's impatient to hear Noriko's verdict ('She must have approved of him. She must have.') and feels that her brother, in his reluctance to push, makes too many allowances.

Seeing Noriko suitably married is a duty for the professor, a sacrifice which is also a relief from the guilt he feels, or at least claims to feel, for monopolising her and holding her back from her own life. So the prospect is wholly sweet for Masa, bitter-sweet for the professor.

In this scene he walks with a stick that hasn't been noticeable before. It's as if even discussing the departure of Noriko from the house has been enough to tip him over into old age. Having married her off, his only remaining task will be to die.

It's only Noriko, unseen but so recently sobbing in front of us, who seems not to understand that she's in a comedy, finding the arrangement bitter and her future dark, with any sense of new beginning swallowed up by a deep reluctance.

As a matter of fact we have seen Professor Somiya walking with his stick before, when he and Noriko left the Noh performance, but then he didn't give an impression of weakness. Perhaps it's partly that in the shrine scene he's relatively casually dressed in the Western style, while Masa is of course in full traditional fig. Is that a cardigan, professor? Normally Somiya holds his own against his formidable sister in matters of dress, whether he wears a kimono or a suit, but here he seems to give a hint, despite the crispness of his open-necked shirt, of the self-neglect of the man who lives alone.

Just as important is the question of footwear. Brother and sister are both wearing the traditional wooden items (though only on him do they look incongruous, clashing with the rest of his casual turnout), neither quite clog nor quite sandal, and looking like miniature coffee tables. If they were sold aggressively to a Western market they would need a new name – clogdals, perhaps.

Their soles are somewhat higher than Western shoes, so that Professor Somiya's smart stick is in effect too short to be brought down fully, without resting weight on it, as part of an easy walking motion. High heels edge the centre of gravity forward, a built-up sole shifts it down. At any event he gives an impression in this sequence of a slight unsteadiness.

I watched the comic scene at the shrine any number of times without noticing a further refinement of the situation. Just before Masa sets off on her pigeon-scattering mission, she turns round and registers alarm at something she sees behind her brother. A moment later he turns round too, and seems equally dismayed by what he sees.

If Ozu had wanted to show us right away what or whom they see behind them, then there was nothing to stop him. (This is the sort of thinking that doesn't seem to get anyone very far in discussions of

*Late Spring.*) Viewers who restrict their attention to the characters they already know, following Masa's brisk progress up the steps, have been given plenty of incongruous entertainment. They're unlikely to feel short-changed. But into the shot at 1:13:04 strolls an official figure, some sort of shrine guard ian or beadle patrolling, dressed in a dark uniform and a cap that make him look like a Western railway porter. He holds his baton of office behind his back. This is self-evidently the right person with whom to deposit a lost item. Taking charge of such matters is an essential part of his job. And Masa legs it. Her coltish burst of energy may partly celebrate her good luck but it also keeps the professor moving forward. As she clatters through the pigeons and up the steps she shows authority, and citizenly ethics, a clean pair of clogdals.

This is broad comedy, close to slapstick, yet Ozu doesn't expect his audience to consume it passively. A certain activeness of response is encouraged. His sensibility retains its fine grain even when his script verges on knockabout.

Noriko has seemed so completely to be excluded from comedy that what we encounter in the next scene is highly surprising: the restoration of her smile. It's the first time we've seen that radiance since the confrontation with Masa, which was nearly half an hour of screen time ago, half a lifetime ago. She's having tea with Aya again, but this time she's almost simpering as she deflects questions about the meeting with Mr Satake. Talk about discontinuity!

'What was he like?'

'My aunt thinks he looks like Gary Cooper.' As if Aunt Masa was now an authority to be invoked with reverence . . .

'Great. You always liked Gary Cooper.'

'But I think he looks more like our local electrician.'

'Does *he* look like Gary Cooper?'

'Yes, very much so.'

This matter of assessing male faces is turning self-referential, tucking inside itself with a half-twist like a Möbius strip. If the local electrician as well as a Tokyo University graduate look like Gary Cooper then there's a lot of star quality about, and the distinction leaks out of the accolade. Admittedly, Hattori doesn't look remotely like Gary Cooper. If there's an American actor of the period whom he resembles, it's Edward G. Robinson on one of his better days.

Aya seems to suspect she's being teased, to judge by her reply ('I'll slap you!' – how characteristically robust). Imagine that, though: Noriko having the confidence to tease Aya on a subject not entirely distant from sex.

Then Aya reverts to another side of her character, the supportive-sisterly: 'But well done for you, trying the marriage meeting . . .

'It sounds good . . .

126

'Don't think too much. Get married! . . .

'There aren't many good ones around. Grab him.'

This new incarnation of Noriko is a very different creature. The sense of having a rich inner life transforms the simplest actions. She even stirs her tea [1:14:15] like a woman with a secret. Her objections to marriage have dwindled almost to a technicality. Suddenly she doesn't mind the idea of living away from her father, and suddenly she forgets the sexual disgust which has been simmering in her character for most of the last hour.

She says, 'I don't like it . . .' – but it turns out that her objection is to arranged marriage, not marriage as such. Aya is understandably impatient with this idea, pointing out that Noriko would never have the nerve to propose.

Aya did the proposing, and look how that turned out. Men are sly, she says, showing only their good side before marriage. It's a different matter afterwards.

It's extraordinary how the balance between the women shifts when Noriko has a little more assurance. Aya's worldly wisdom begins to seem very hollow. The argument that men can hide their true natures obviously applies just as much (if not more) to arranged marriages, which leads Aya to propose that Noriko marries Satake on principle and then leaves him if she doesn't like their life together. The worst of both worlds, the formality of a family introduction without any confidence in the result. No wonder Noriko laughs at the idea.

Is it just the formal fact that Noriko has an acknowledged suitor that changes her manner? When Aya comes up with truths about life – 'Love doesn't always mean a happy marriage', for instance – Noriko just smiles enigmatically and says 'I wonder.' When Aya offers tips on how to make things work between a man and a woman – 'All you need to do is to smile at him. He'll fall for you . . . then you take control' – Noriko says 'No way' with another little laugh. Challenged on her home (though very precarious) ground of marital knowledge, Aya insists: 'That's how it works. Do you think I'm joking?' Again Noriko says merely, 'I wonder.' It's as if she knows more about life than Aya, all of a sudden, and is indulging her deluded friend.

It's a disorienting little encounter. After a whole series of scenes showing that the prospect of getting married pushes Noriko close to mental and emotional collapse, this much lighter conversation seems less like a development of the dramatic situation than a variation on a theme of general interest, young women's attitudes to marriage. Like the sequences suggesting that Noriko has an interest in Hattori despite everything she's said, it doesn't harmonise with the central presentation of the character, even actively contradicts it. In the editing suite of memory, when a version of the film is assembled for the archives, these lengths of subtly discrepant footage are likely to flutter disregarded to the floor. Surplus jigsaw pieces need to be tipped out of the box with a sort of superstitious haste, before they call into question the coherence of the whole picture.

If it's positively eerie to see Noriko apparently full of confidence in her sexual status as a woman with a suitor, preening herself ('He used to play basketball when he was a student') about the desirability of the man whose arrival in her life she has to date greeted only with horror, it's also unnerving to see Aunt Masa nervous in the next scene, when she and the professor wait for Noriko to return home and deliver her answer to the proposed marriage.

Of course Masa's nerves are understandable. Her scheme for tidying up the family hasn't met with the co-operation it deserves. The very fact that she is waiting for Noriko to have the good manners to return from a day out in Tokyo shows that things aren't running smoothly. In the meantime she gives vent to some strange thoughts. Could Noriko be bothered by trivial things?

By this she means her suitor's name, Kumatoro Satake, since apparently Kumatoro would mean 'the bear boy'. Her brother thinks it's a good name, a strong name, but she has her doubts. 'Doesn't it make you think of a thick, hairy chest?' she asks, making a gesture of fascinated disgust towards her own upper body. It's as if the infestation of sexual queasiness which Noriko seemed to throw off in the previous scene, needing a new host, has migrated to her.

Professor Somiya gives a chuckle signifying assenting dissent or agreeable disagreement. Really, it's astonishing how many non-committal noises Chishu Ryu has at his disposal – even when he was confirming Noriko's fears about his remarrying he sounded as if he was hedging his bets, or keeping his fingers crossed out of sight to neutralise a lie.

Masa insists that these things do bother young girls (things such as names suggesting animal appetites) but of course she's the one who is bothered, as she now admits, about the difficulty of finding a suitable familiar form of name for this person who will, if things go to plan, become part of her family. Kumatoro-san sounds crude, Kuma-san is impossibly common and Kuma-chan is even worse. She decides on Ku-chan. What does he think? He gives a neutral growl that could mean anything.

Some people use pet names and diminutives as a way of confirming their own sense of control. Perhaps it's significant that the form of words Masa has chosen for Noriko's husband-to-be is so close to the familiar name for her own son (Bu-chan).

Noriko's back. Aunt Masa says something meant to be overheard, something that's supposed to convey that they haven't been talking about the only subject Masa cares about ('Well, that was when . . .') though Noriko is probably past the point of caring about such niceties. Noriko walks through the shot and out of their sight, heading for her own room. She's not visibly upset, but there is nothing left of the animation she showed when talking to Aya about basketball and film stars.

'How is she?' Masa asks her brother, but he just makes one of his noises, mammalian but not necessarily human. You might as well try to decide whether a sea-lion has just said 'please' or 'thank you'.

Aunt Masa promises him that she'll be tactful with Noriko, then follows her upstairs. If the teenager has yet to be invented, so too has the privacy of a dependant's bedroom.

The scene between niece and aunt which follows is a painful study in passive resistance, with Noriko trying to shut Masa out of the conversation so as to deny her the knowledge of her triumph. The decision isn't real until it has been passed on. There's a sense in which it hasn't even happened yet, as long as she can put off the moment of admitting it.

In previous scenes with her father Noriko has withheld both eye contact and answers to questions, but in the previous confrontation with Masa she didn't dare attempt this double defiance. She did all she could to keep her eyes occupied elsewhere, but she didn't actively impede conversation. Now she does.

Masa's opening gambit is to say, 'Oh, welcome home, Nori-chan.' Everything about this is contemptible: the attempt to have a conversation in Noriko's own room when she showed she had no taste for it in the social spaces downstairs, the smarmy use of the familiar form, the idea of a non-resident welcoming a resident, particularly as Masa's whole scheme is to tranfer her to an unknown address elsewhere. Noriko's 'Hello' is distant and cold.

Masa can't help herself going on with 'Well, about that meeting . . .' At this point Noriko gets under way with some little domestic routines that enable her to ignore her aunt without blatant rudeness. Who could object to a well-brought-up young woman attending to the maintenance of her clothes? It's best not to put off such tasks, since slovenliness is the long-term result of any procrastinating tendency. Noriko has found a little enclave of indemnity, and can turn her back on Masa in all innocence while she puts her jacket on a hanger.

Masa is stranded and must give her a further prompt: 'Have you thought about it?' Again Noriko declines to engage with her aunt. For a few precious moments more, Masa is both invisible and inaudible.

Masa is a meddler and a pain in the neck, but she's not a fool. She understands that there are other ways of entering into conversation than having your questions answered. Her next gambit attempts to align her with Noriko's current set of grooming actions, and so give her some sneaky access to the routines that are being used to exclude her. When

Noriko turns (still not making eye contact), apparently in search of something on the table, Masa strikes like a snake [1:18:01], picking up a stray hanky and offering it to her.

This ploy isn't a great success. It turns out that Noriko wasn't looking for a hanky at all. She reaches down to a lower storage level of the the table and retrieves a hair brush, not looking at Masa or otherwise acknowledging her helpfulness. Masa seems continually to be pressing unwanted objects on her niece, and wanting to be thanked for her trouble. If it isn't a husband it's a hanky.

Noriko moves into the corridor and starts brushing her jacket. Masa follows her out and stands behind her, oppressively close. She presses the point: 'Haven't you?'

Noriko turns and walks away, giving the brush a couple of swift strokes against her skirt as if to dislodge some fluff. Then she goes back into her room. If throwing cloth around is the only critically authorised way for Ozu's women to express their darker emotions, then dislodging imaginary fluff is pretty small beer – but perhaps she's imagining Masa in the role of the fluff.

Back in her room Noriko consolidates her composure by imposing some order on her possessions. She hangs up the jacket, takes up her handbag and retrieves the hanky. Masa says, 'I think it's a splendid arrangement, don't you?'

Noriko has run out of things to do with her hands, excuses for not responding, but she manages to stay silent a little longer. She sits down in the chair where we saw her weeping so bitterly in a previous scene after her father had left, and turns her face half away. This seems to have become her designated misery chair. She first took her sorrows there in the scene of bath rejection, when she returned distraught from her aunt's.

Masa doesn't let up. 'Well, will you marry him?'

'. . .'

'Say something.'

Finally Noriko say 'Yes' in a flat voice. Under pressure from her father, she was able to ignore eight conversational openings. Now, with Masa, she can manage to ignore only six. Still an impressive display of non-cooperation from a well-brought-up young woman – but her strength is running out.

Masa takes some time to absorb the news, partly because Noriko's resistance has been protracted, and partly because her manner is now so crushed. Masa beams, but Noriko's face reflects none of that elation back to her.

Masa leaves at high speed, as if she was afraid that Noriko might change her mind. On the way out she picks up something from the floor and puts it, as it were, 'helpfully' on the table. It might be another hanky. Masa has a genius for spotting them. Everything she does is 'helpful', and the inverted commas are an integral part of her particular style of making her presence felt.

It's possible that on some subliminal level Noriko's symbolic movement of brushing away fluff has registered on Masa. Downstairs, spilling over with satisfaction, doing everything to express her delight short of leading a conga-dance round the room, she finds time to flick something off the professor's kimono. It's the sort of gesture that lays a claim rather than offers a service. She conveys by it that her brother can't look after himself, and perhaps she's looking forward to her next bit of family tidying, when the link with Mrs Miwa will (as she must imagine) be firmly established with her indispensable assistance.

It's during this celebratory conversation with her brother downstairs that Masa reveals that she's still got the purse she helped herself to earlier. He seems quite shocked by a dilatoriness crossing over into actual dishonesty.

Isn't he putting it on a bit, though? The time to register a protest was earlier, when there was a shrine beadle in earshot, not now, when it would take a certain amount of effort to deposit the wallet with the authorities, on its highly theoretical way to being reunited with its owner. There's some bad faith involved on Somiya's part, or a little bit of denial. If he doesn't know what Masa is like by now, then it's because he'd rather not.

This sort of psychological speculation about the

unreal people on the screen has no objective force, but it's a major part of what has made cinema such an enduring phenomenon, the sense of interaction with something incapable of interacting.

On her way out (if she hurries she can catch the 9.35 train) Masa says that she won't lock the door. Why on earth should she? How does she imagine the household functions when she's not around? (Since Ozu has omitted to include technical drawings of Japanese locks, or even close-ups, I have to assume something like the snib of a Yale lock, allowing people to lock a door on their way out without the use of a key.) Here she is 'tactfully' drawing her brother's attention to the need for security, and rather less tactfully revealing that in her view he needs steering in the simplest aspects of life.

When she has left, the professor sits down on the floor again, his face expressing a certain amount of satisfaction (if only on the level of 'at least *that*'s over'). Perhaps he's still bathed in the afterglow of Masa's triumph, complicated by a twinge of the loneliness he anticipates for himself.

Noriko comes downstairs, almost sidling round the corner into the room. She picks up something from a cabinet, paying the bare minimum of attention to her father and keeping her eyes on the floor in front of her feet. This isn't encouraging. Logically you would expect Noriko's face to be the primary radiant source of joy in the family, Masa's merely a dutiful mirror of it, but with Masa's departure all sense of satisfaction seems to have left the house.

'Your aunt just left.'

'Did she?' Without much interest.

'She was really happy.'

Noriko picks up a pot that's sitting on a low table and undertakes some mildly mysterious business with it, remaining turned away from him. He asks, 'Are you sure about your answer?'

In the next shot she seems to be counting something out in the palm of her hand. 'Yes,' she says, still without turning round.

'It's not like you're giving up, are you?'

'No'. Still not turning round.

'You're not reluctant, are you?'

This time she does turn round, to show him a face that seems to be seething with contempt. 'No, I'm not.' Sending a message not far from *How stupid are you*? If you can't see the truth when it's staring you in the face, why expect to be told?

In time the vocabulary of family conflict will expand as the conventions take hold, both nationally and internationally. In that future period such phrases as 'I'm fine', spoken in a voice near tears, will rarely be mistaken for the end of a conversation.

'I see,' says her father. 'Then that's alright.'

She turns away without a word, leaving him puzzled and unhappy. He lifts his tea- or *sake*-cup up onto the table.

This is the second time that Noriko has come downstairs for no overwhelming reason, at a moment when her emotional state would seem to dictate a preference for solitude. Personally I find the earlier scene the less plausible of the two. This time her mood is closer to resignation than desolate sorrow, and her errand is more cogent. In the earlier scene, she came downstairs in search of some bath product or other, now she is looking for an unspecified pot. What she counts out in the palm of her hand may be pills – the shot is too short to allow of certainty – and the medicine chest outranks the cosmetics drawer. Noriko had a hospital appointment early in the film, after all (at which she was given a clean bill of health), though if that hint is followed up in the film it's only here.

There's no obvious reason, in either scene, for the professor not to go up to Noriko in her room. He wouldn't need the pretext of being in search for a container of any sort. Yet Ozu, to put it mildly, knows what he's doing. If he decides against the father seeking out the daughter he has a reason for it. The reason may be the importance for him of making clear that this is not a film about arranged marriage, and therefore to avoid scenes in which the father might appear to be applying pressure, even of the tenderest and most loving kind.

Of course, the whole business of examining a film frame by frame, as I have been doing, to try to fix the identity of an object or the meaning of a movement, is wildly artificial and only recently possible in terms of technology. It enables the public at large to play director, which in movie terms is no different from playing God.

To film-goers of my generation the formal distinction between cinema and theatre, that a filmed product can be repeated on demand, was pretty much a technicality. The difference was probably better expressed (to cinema's disadvantage) by saying that film-goers had never actually been in the same room as the people they were watching.

Repeatability wasn't an easy option before the days of videotape. If you missed a film on its first run you had to join a film club or wait for a re-release. When for instance I caught up with *Lawrence of Arabia* it was at a college film society screening in some common room of modest size. I remember being unimpressed by the fussy camera movements, not realising at the time that in a doomed attempt to emphasise the humanly dramatic part of each frame, and to scale it up, this version had been cropped, the vast distances between characters bridged by imposed panning within the image, so that the desert itself (surely a dominant character in the drama) hardly got a look in. What I saw was more like *Lawrence of Centerparcs* than what David Lean intended.

So the remarkable thing is not that a couple of scenes in *Late Spring* fall short of total implausibility, but that the film as a whole holds up to viewing after viewing, revealing riches without loss of mystery. The film offers a stream of charged gestures and encounters with expressive objects. The characters reveal themselves as much as by any other means through their interactions with clothes, furniture, domestic spaces, hair-brushes, towels, hankies and stray threads.

If you had read about Ozu's style and preoccupations before seeing any of his films, before seeing *Late Spring*, you would be expecting something like a Vermeer with the bonus of some stately movement. What you get, if you allow yourself to notice, is something more like micro-sociology, a close examination of the way manners mesh with morals, or fail to, in the way people perform their lives, while also under certain circumstances distancing themselves from their roles.

Micro-sociology was the brainchild of Erving Goffman, whose classic first book, *The Presentation of Self in Everyday Life*, was published in 1959, ten years after *Late Spring*. Goffman identified the importance for complex social play, the theatre of daily life, of backstage areas (such as hotel kitchens, Goffman's 'fieldwork' in this area being done in the Shetlands), of thresholds and other intermediate spaces. His signature insight (if chefs have signature dishes, sociologists should certainly be given parity) was that most of our actions in social space are like bits of stage 'business', the acting out of our responses in stylised form. A classic example would be the way that, having spotted a friend on the street some way off, we abstain from eye contact until we can 'recognise' and greet them properly at close quarters. Anyone who consistently behaved with more truth fulness, waving from the middle distance and keeping up a steady barrage of smiles until the point at which a conversation free of shouting became possible, would not long pass for sane.

Goffman's analyses don't cross cultures with any guaranteed smoothness, and he assumes a certain amount of social stability underpinning individual anxieties about status and dignity. The Japan of *Late Spring*, of course, was still adjusting to the aftershocks of upheaval, and the recent replacement of a theocratic militarism by a democracy that no one had voted for.

It would be nice to think that the tablecloth of the constitution could be yanked deftly away from under the place settings of family life, leaving everything in its place. But the part played by the constitution in this analogy is the table and not the tablecloth.

To get a flavour of the difference between cultures which the new constitution set out to harmonise, it's not realistic to scrutinise films of the immediate postwar period, which were hardly likely to portray any underlying conflict or incomprehension. Later films can be more direct. Perhaps a remark by a character in *The Catch,* a 1961 film by Nagisa Oshima, who lived through the war (though not as an adult) gives some idea. 'Do the Americans think Japanese are bad people?' he asks. At this point in the film, the Emperor has surrendered and the war is over. 'Do the Americans think Japanese are bad people?' It's a protest against the occupation, for which there was no need. Do the Americans think Japanese are bad people?

As the speaker goes on to explain, after the surrender of the Emperor it would be impossible for any Japanese to continue fighting. Only bad people, which the Japanese are not, would defy their Emperor by resisting. According to this view of the world the American occupation is not a military or political necessity but simply an insult to the character of the Japanese people, who were not fighting, killing and dying in the first person but acting entirely as instruments of their Emperor. It's not a reading of reality which could make sense to a member of the occupying forces.

Decorously *Late Spring* turns its eyes away from such things, but just the same its characters live in a world where the fixed points have been melted down. Fathers no longer command, sacrifice is no longer an official principle, but of the people we see in the film only Aya seems to have signed up, with real enthusiasm but mixed results, to the new ways of being.

142

Professor Somiya and Noriko are more divided, internally and from each other's adjustments. Every now and again it can seem that the face work between father and daughter has somehow misfired, failing to convey the required information. 'Face work' – that's a technical term of Goffmanian analysis, which I've appropriated with the wilful slackness of my dilettante breed.

The moments of potential misunderstanding, misaligned hinges of communication, come first when Noriko presses her father to confirm that he plans to marry Mrs Miwa, and then when Professor Somiya seeks to be reassured that Noriko is really following her own desires in agreeing to accept the match proposed for her. In the first case, the tentative nature of the signals he sends, those so nearly neutral gruntlets and half-nods, would normally be enough to telegraph a lack of conviction, except that Noriko's sense of betrayal, of her worst fears being realised, didn't override her common sense.

In the second conversation, it isn't the weakness of the signals but their dissonance which should set the alarm bells ringing. Noriko's words and her expression contradict each other. She's like a hostage on camera saying that everything's fine, but rolling her eyes discreetly to convey that there's a gun trained on her out of shot. Yet everyone agrees she's a free agent. She says so herself, and goes on acting as if she was under the gun.

She and her father seem to be caught in an *enryo* trap, as surely as Cyril and Cecil, the polite English twins in the womb, neither of them able to make a salutary selfish choice.

There's no possible reason for the 'three-act' structure that still turns up in so much Hollywood product to have any bearing on Japanese cinema, but it's true that *Late Spring* has something of that patterning placement of two intervals. The first interval arrived unannounced after Noriko in her first turmoil fled the house, with the action resuming only at the Noh. Now there is a gap of time and tone between the shot of Professor Somiya baffled by Noriko's mixed messages and what comes next, the trip to Kyoto, the farewell tour of the father-daughter bond, under notice of termination yet holding.

The visit to Kyoto has come to be regarded as the bittersweet highlight of the film, leading up as it does to That Vase, but that's not how it seems to the first-time viewer. There's just an unexplained change of scenery. No physical destination or emotional script has been announced. Everything has to be reconstructed by the viewer, and it falsifies the film to skip over that stage, as if it wasn't important. Ozu could perfectly well have inserted a bit of dialogue to establish the necessary information, either as part of the last scene or in a trifling addition to the narrative – the professor hesitantly going upstairs to suggest it, bearing an olive branch without really understanding why one is needed.

If Ozu chose to leave us in the dark, let's assume he had his reasons. We're meant to pass abruptly from a position of imagined superior knowledge, mildly shocked that a kindly father could be so blind, to a state of knowing much less than the characters. The way the film destabilises our dealings with it is a major part of the cinematic machinery, but goes for nothing if audiences are primed for *bittersweet farewell visit to Kyoto* from the first frame, if not before.

What do we actually see? A view of a hilltop, and the pinnacle of a pagoda-like building. Another shot of the same building, showing several levels of the stylised stacking of the roof. A closer shot of the same. Perhaps, to Japanese eyes, as blatant a way of signalling 'Kyoto' as the Hattori building is of announcing 'Tokyo', but not necessarily legible at a greater cultural distance. Less specific but more informative, in that it clearly suggests travel, is the next shot, of suitcases, with a man's hat perched on one of them, and a suit hung tidily up.

Noriko and her father are in the bathroom of their hotel room, and her smile is back in place. Not only that, but the spirit of co-operation seems to be in force again and working its familiar magic at this temporary address. Noriko hands the professor his tooth-glass so that he can rinse. She folds a small towel. They discuss the ease of the train journey with an accompanying body language that is both fluent and relaxed.

This present-tense aspect of their relationship has been missing from the moment that Aunt Masa unveiled her schemes to Noriko. Since then there has been no sharing of food or drink, no tender tidying or anticipation of needs. The fabric of the household was rent across in an instant, damaged apparently beyond repair, but now it has been re-constituted for a little while in this impermanent environment. Seedlings of domestic harmony have been replanted in their hotel room.

Even so, the new growth isn't exactly vigorous. These gestures are slight in terms of their actual usefulness. A person who hands a tooth-glass to an-other is conveying something that was already within reach – and if there is any setting in which towel-folding can be dispensed with, it's surely the hotel bathroom. These services rendered by Noriko to her father are almost wholly symbolic. They memorialise a relationship as much as they keep one alive.

After a near-ethnographic shot of women in the street with baskets on their heads, presumably to in-dicate the picturesque old ways of Kyoto, the camera shows us a man from behind, smoking. This turns out to be Onodera, absent from the film since Noriko invited him to dinner, after she had seemed to insult him for his unclean behaviour in marrying again.

Professor Somiya enters, followed by Noriko, apologising for keeping Onodera waiting. Is it just me, or is it odd to keep a visitor waiting while you brush your teeth and discuss your journey? I can't help feeling that Noriko could be spared from tooth-glass and hand-towel duties to take on the responsibility of greeting Onodera. Some continuity business with textiles certainly makes it seem that this scene follows directly from the previous one – the professor is drying his hands on the little towel as he enters the room. Then he hands it to Noriko, who seems to be carrying quite a little collection of bathroom requisites, three cloth items in all. She goes out of shot to put at least some of them away.

Onodera says, 'I'm glad you came.' The professor makes one of his trademark noises – the gearbox in his throat seems to be stuck in neutral. He takes out a cigarette and prepares to smoke it, squashing the end with his lips to make a sort of mouthpiece. It's the first time he's managed without a holder. Perhaps he left it at home. It may be that Noriko hid it from him while he was packing, to avoid any possibility of his performing that embarrassing nose-stroking trick of his in front of strangers, in a holy city.

'Noriko's getting married soon,' he says.

'Really?' says Onodera, sounding no more than mildly interested.

147

'This is our last trip together.'

Onodera does a little better. 'Oh, congratulations! That's wonderful news.' Up to this point he has been addressing the professor, but now he turns towards Noriko and says again, 'Congratulations.'

Noriko is sitting on a cushion, apparently light-hearted and unconcerned. She divides her attention between the conversation and playing with a cloth object of some sort. It might be a folded hand towel, the same or another, even a recurrence of the hanky theme. Oh dear, I'm rather at sea with Japanese haberdashery of the immediate post-war period. No doubt there's a website.

Whatever the object is, Noriko repeatedly throws it up in the air a few inches and catches it. At one stage during the conversation that follows she lets it rotate fully in mid-air, end to end, in the manner of a pancake chef, before she catches it again.

Onodera makes jocular remarks about Noriko's intended: 'What is he like compared to me?' It's her father, though, who answers on her behalf, saying 'There's no comparison.'

Portly, middle-aged Onodera courts embarrassment by pressing the point. 'Who's better?'

This time Noriko answers for herself. 'Of course, you're much nicer.' Not better, but nicer. I doubt if there's a significant distinction being made.

Onodera offers to buy them lunch, saying that Misako (his daughter) wants to see Noriko, but giving warning that 'the unclean one', his new wife, will also be there. Noriko laughs without much in the way of embarrassment, unfolds what she's been playing with – it seems be made of a very fine embroidered fabric, like a voile – and hangs it up.

(For some reason Onodera's daughter, in both the versions I've seen, starts the film as Isako, or just Isa, and ends it as Misako.)

This game with the towel is rather unlike anything we have seen Noriko do in the rest of the film. When she's with Aya, particularly in their first scene together, and with Hattori at the beach, she can indulge in banter and teasing, but this absorption in play with an object is different. She seems to be acting out with calculation the spontaneous behaviour of 'a carefree girl'. The routine of throwing and catching is part of that performance, and has the added benefit of allowing her to make eye contact only intermittently without the risk of seeming rude. It's much easier to play a part when you don't have to look at your audience the whole time.

To some extent she miscalculates her display of childlike mannerism. She seems to be regressing rather than moving towards maturity as might be expected, now that she is about to cast off her single state and enter the consecrated domain of marriage.

Her artificial childlikeness casts a light back on the scene of her waiting on her father in the bathroom with tooth-glass and towel. The slight exaggeration of her ministrations suggest the child playing at being helpful rather than actually helping, a child for whom suitably undemanding tasks must be invented.

Despite the communal-sounding arrangements (Onodera's 'How about lunch today?'), we next see the professor talking to a woman in traditional dress, perhaps the guide to a shrine, while Noriko spends time with Onodera and his daughter.

The conversation with the shrine guide, if that's what she is, is pretty much small talk ('Do you come to Kyoto often, professor?' – which at least lets us know the scene of the action). Monkish chanting and a drum beat become audible under the music. The professor is wearing a formal Western suit, and again sports a stick. 'Sporting' seems to be the right word for it, since his smart turn-out transforms the stick into something closer to a status symbol than an aid to weakness. He doesn't seem to be putting any weight on it. Of course, Professor Somiya wouldn't be the first man in history to experience an involuntary improvement of posture in the company of an unfamiliar young woman, however innocently of flirtatious intention.

There's a cry of 'Uncle!' on the soundtrack, as Misako shouts for his attention from a nearby terrace, where she's standing with Noriko and her father. He waves back, and then we see the three of them from behind.

Three, not four. The potentially awkward conversation with 'the unclean one' has already taken place, but though we have been excluded from what promised to be an important conversation the issue is still rumbling on. The tone, though, since it is set by Onodera, is boisterously comic. 'Noriko,' he says, 'how do you feel about the unclean?'

She seems a bit thrown, and replies with a reproachful 'You're so mean.'

Mean or not, Onodera won't be put off. 'Tell me what you think.'

Misako intervenes to ask her father what being labelled as 'unclean' means. Though she's no longer a child (twenty-five and 'refusing to get married' as her father indicated early in the film), the question has a childish innocence to it. Depending on how beleaguered Noriko feels, Misako's intervention is either a reprieve, putting Onodera in the spotlight for a change, or an intensification of the general discomfort.

'Hm? It's filthy. Right, Noriko?' It doesn't take Onodera long to put the ball back in her court.

Noriko turns, and gives him a playful slap on the arm. She seems to have recovered her poise, though she walks smartly off while he laughs. In the next shot, more or less from the professor's middle-distance point of view, we see that she has moved a little further across the terrace and is leaning on a railing, 'admiring the view'.

This standby of tourists everywhere doesn't gain her much breathing space. Onodera pesters her further with his drollery. Again she play-slaps him, this time on the back, before going back towards the daughter. It isn't easy to decipher Noriko's manner at this distance, but she lowers her head, perhaps in laughter, whether real or assumed.

We're already located in what might be the professor's point of view, but the next shot (from a similar angle) shows him and his companion looking in another direction, admiring the view without self-consciousness, with the implication that he hasn't been a witness to this byplay. The professor turns and waves, and the two groups move towards each other out of shot.

We don't see them converge. Instead there's a transitional shot of a group of schoolgirls, and of an ornamental water pipe discharging into a pond.

Only now do I realise that the woman talking with Professor Somiya, displaying the animated indifference of tour guides worldwide, may be (must be?) the second Mrs Onodera.

No one could be less like a scarlet woman than this earnest, almost fawning costume doll. If she's really married to bouncy, facetious Onodera then it's a marriage of opposites. She's as chalky as he is cheesy. It seems appropriate that they should be geographically separated in this scene, far removed from each other even when technically present in the same frame. Theirs is hardly likely to be an arranged marriage, but nor does it seem a possible love match. There's no common ground between them in manner or costume, between the failed formality of a rumpled suit (topped off with a cloth cap and a Chaplinesque cane) and the untouchability of traditional dress. It's certainly easier to imagine Noriko's behaviour in the omitted scene of introductions than any possible byplay between such a husband and wife. That will have to be my excuse for being so slow on the uptake.

What with Westernised, confrontational Aya and jokey, tactless Onodera, you could say that Noriko pretty much has to run the gauntlet of the film's more direct conversationalists, but perhaps there is more to Onodera's manner in the scene just past than its surface tactlessness. For one thing his buffoonish manner, with its abdication from any adult dignity, takes the sting out of the situation. It even licenses Noriko to respond childishly herself, with her play-slaps and little stylised dashes across the terrace. Though she is an adult and about to prove it by getting married, she can remain cocooned in the position of the child who pronounces certain subjects nasty, without needing to give a reason.

Onodera has also shifted the ground of the controversy. Noriko didn't say anything about his second wife, just that he was filthy for remarrying. The unclean one was always him, not her. It would be exaggerating to say that Noriko has a philosophy of sexuality, but it does seem clear that she regards it as a male shortcoming, imposed on women without their bearing responsibility.

The immediate question about this scene is: whose sensibilities is Odonera protecting with this sly change of emphasis? He might be saving Noriko embarrassment by locating the awkwardness a little further away, or he might be exonerating himself from the misremembered slur.

The scene we don't see, the one with Onodera's new wife taking part, might settle the question, and might not. In any case its omission fits a larger and very characteristic pattern in *Late Spring*, of not showing couples interacting. Hattori's fiancée doesn't appear except as a photograph, though she's a friend of Noriko's. We don't see Noriko's suitor, Mr Satake. Nor do we see Noriko's uncle, the man who could tame Aunt Masa, or alternatively not feel the need to. The only functioning partnership we see is the one between father and daughter, the partnership whose severing is the story of the film.

In the next scene, the two of them are in their hotel room on the last night of their excursion to Kyoto, ready for bed, the professor cross-legged and smoking a cigarette. Noriko rubs her hands together slowly, looking off at a dreamy angle in an attitude that is almost Garboesque. If the action was faster her hand-movements would approximate to 'wringing the hands' and seem anxious or guilty, but I doubt if that's the implication. Perhaps it's just that as part of her bedtime ritual she has put some cream on them.

The professor rubs at his left leg, saying 'We walked a lot today. Aren't you tired?'

'No,' says Noriko, and her smile as she turns towards him is as radiant as it has ever been.

He goes on, 'The last time I was here, the bush-clover was magnificent.' Noriko looks at her hands held in front of her, palms up, as if she was cradling a precious, invisible book. Then she strokes one hand with the other, looking at the palm with serene intentness. She may only be checking that her hand cream has been fully absorbed by the skin.

They discuss their plans for the next day. Onodera's daughter Misako will come to see Noriko at ten. They'll go to the museum. Noriko laces her fingers together, but without showing the tension or uncertainty which that gesture can sometimes express. There's a vase on the floor behind her.

The professor suggests that they go to sleep, and Noriko agrees, volunteering to turn off the light. She stands up to do so, using a switch we don't see. Soft shadowed light comes in through the window-screens, projecting silhouettes of foliage stirred by a breeze. It's a magical change of emphasis, the artificial light taken away without total loss of visibility and with a great gain in atmosphere. In semi-darkness, with the presence of nature and moving air outside, the room seems to have expanded. This might be a good moment to give the name of the film's director of photography, Yuharu Atsuta.

They settle down in their beds. 'Well . . .' says Noriko tentatively, but stops there. 'Yes?' prompts her father. The shot changes, so that we're looking at her from his side.

'I'm afraid I was very rude to Uncle Onodera.'

'Why?' This subtitle isn't helpful. It isn't clear whether it means 'Why do you say so?' or 'Why were you rude?', though the first meaning seems more likely.

'His wife is such a nice person. They make a wonderful couple. I shouldn't have called him unclean.'

Not much fudging of issues here, or only secondary fudging. Noriko is in no doubt that she insulted Onodera rather than his wife, but it's not clear whether the niceness of the chosen woman, or even their alleged complementary virtue as a couple, has the power to neutralise her reaction. It had seemed to be a primal revulsion rather than anything as thought-through as disapproval.

Professor Somiya reassures her that there was no offence taken.

Noriko makes another tentative opening. 'Father . . . I had been feeling unpleasant about your case . . .' She turns towards him, her smile dying away, as if she was about to make some long-delayed confession.

He's asleep, securely propped up on his neck-pillow. She turns her head away from him, so that she seems to be looking at the ceiling, then part of the way back towards him. We hear him snoring faintly.

This is where the vase shot comes in. You won't believe me if I say it lasts six seconds, and I'm probably cheating a bit. Back to a shot of her face. She moves her head slightly to the side away from her father, then back, her eyelids drooping faintly. She blinks.

Then the vase shot returns, held for even longer, ten full seconds, to the accompaniment of the professor's gentle snores.

There's no sign of tears (Paul Schrader), or their nearness (Donald Richie), but it seems silly to be stern. Only in an age of digital media can footage be scrutinised more or less to forensic standards. If these critics get tears or near-tears then so be it, even if their testimony wouldn't stand up under cross-examination. A piece of film criticism isn't a statement in court.

I'm not sure it's even a problem that from Noriko's position lying in bed, she can't possibly be looking at the vase we see. Film language is more elastic than that, and Ozu's particular brand of it is as stretchy as flubber knickers. If it's the same vase that appeared in shot earlier in the sequence, then it's actually behind her. It isn't exactly a moment of shock (along the lines of the homicidal dwarf at the end of *Don't Look Now* having lurked in the hero's slide collection from the very beginning) if it turns out there's only the one vase rather than two.

It's a shame that the term 'pillow shot' is such a disputed critical term. Otherwise the timeless moment with the vase would qualify (since Noriko is lying on one at the time) as the pillow shot to end all pillow shots.

Apparently Ozu was quite a connoisseur of fine textiles and ceramics, and often used items from his own collection as props to dress the sets of his films. For all I know the vase in this shot was a particular treasure of his. Still I resist the attempt to turn him into a humdrum aesthete, as Yamada Sokae does in an article from 2002, admiring 'the totalizing obsession with tiny detail, the fetishistic arrangements of favorite objects such as props and actors in space, the unending quest for refinement and the perfect collection, and a love of display combined with an obstinate indifference to the significance others might find in the collection's arrangement and composition'. Better a Zen mage than a refugee from the *Antiques Roadshow*.

The flexibility of Ozu's procedures is demonstrated by the next shot: a Zen garden of raked gravel, dominated by a pair of boulders to the left and right. A 'pillow shot' – or at least an interlude, charged with stillness, between scenes. In this case the boulders seem faintly reminiscent of what we have just seen, as if Noriko, seeming to reach some sort of acceptance, and her father, transcendentally snoring, were being recapitulated in mineral form, magically passing through the imagination of Henry Moore. Then the shot changes to show the boulders in a more central position, formally framed.

Next we see Professor Somiya and Onodera sitting side by side, formally dressed in Western clothes, on a verandah. The echo of the boulders is pretty faint – but then we see that the verandah actually overlooks the Zen garden in the previous shots. So though what we have been watching corresponds to that possibly chimerical thing the pillow shot, it's also a variation on that very dull element of classic Hollywood film language, the establishing shot (showing us where the action takes place). It's a famous garden, apparently, the Ryoanji garden.

Possibly the linking shots are more inventive than the scene they introduce, a conversation between the men about daughters, with Onodera saying 'I'm amazed you finally decided to let her go' and neutral grunts on both sides. The professor says that sons are better than daughters, because you have to let daughters go. The two of them laugh together, fairly unconvincingly.

Ozu gets some more mileage out of the gravel-and-boulder garden, cutting back to it and then back to the men. The sequence ends with two long-held shots of the garden – in fact they're roughly the same length as the two shots of the vase in the previous scene, though no one has ever claimed to detect any similar revelations of transience here, any strong whiffs of *mono-no-aware*.

If I had to nominate a point in the film when it seems to be running out of steam, this would be my choice, but Ozu always has surprises up his sleeve, whether he's wearing a kimono or Western dress.

Next we're back in the hotel watching father and daughter do their packing. Professor Somiya packs books, Noriko packs (what else?) items of cloth. He refers to how short a time they've had away, and she turns towards him, smiling at full power, and says 'Yes . . . but I really enjoyed Kyoto.' That smile of hers is a positive Sarah Bernhardt, returning after every farewell tour refreshed and ready for another.

'I'm glad we came,' he says, on a soothing, cooing note. A little later in the conversation he says, 'Why didn't we do this more often together?' At last he's moved from book-packing to his own bit of towel-folding. 'This is our last trip together.'

At this point Noriko, who has been briskly folding a pair of stockings, slows right down. Her smile disappears, though it comes back after a few moments lacking something of its full complement of brightness. The smile comes back again just at the moment her father turns towards her. She's not looking at him, but it's as if she is able to sense, prompted only by her peripheral vision, the need to restore normal service in terms of facial expression.

'You'll be busy when we get home,' says the professor. 'Your aunt is waiting.' Then, after a moment, 'I hope we'll find seats on the train . . .'

Her movements have come almost to a stop, as if she is nerving herself to go through with something she's decided to do.

He looks at one of his books, saying cheerfully, 'I couldn't take you many places but your husband will. He will take good care of you.' Then he turns towards her, and what he sees on her face makes him hesitate. 'What is it?'

She's looking into the distance and says nothing. 'Is anything wrong?'

She starts to say something but breaks off. 'I . . .'

He makes a soft noise of encouragement, without the benefit of subtitles. She looks at him and says, 'I want to be with you like this.'

He looks baffled.

'I don't want to go anywhere. I'm happy being with you like this.'

Ozu changes to a wider shot that shows them both. She goes on: 'I'm happy just as I am . . . Marriage wouldn't make me any happier.' She links the fingers of her hands and looks down at them.

Her father starts saying, 'But, you see . . .' and she interrupts tenderly to say, 'No. no. You can remarry, Father. But I want to be at your side . . . I

161

love you very much . . . My greatest happiness is to be with you.'

She reaches out a hand towards him as she says, 'Please, Father. Why can't we stay as we are?' Her voice is soft and cajoling.

A new shot of her, a medium close-up, as she meets her father's eyes slightly to the right of us. 'I don't think marriage will make me any happier.'

He says, almost fiercely, 'That's not true.' Though still pretty mild, it's his most combative moment in the whole film.

Then, with a slight return of his usual smile, 'It's nothing like that . . . I'm already fifty-six. My life is nearing its end. Yours is just beginning. Your life is just about to start. A life which you and Satake will build together.'

She looks down into her lap, at one hand covering the other, while he says, 'A life apart from me. That is how humans and history carry on . . .' This is where he launches into it at last, the worst pre-nuptial pep talk the world has ever seen.

'Marriage may not bring happiness from the start . . . It's wrong to think that marriage will instantly make you happy.' To judge from her face, this isn't what she's thinking. 'Happiness is not a thing to wait for, but what you create. Happiness is not about getting married. Happiness lies in the couple creating a new life together . . . It may take a year or two . . . or even five, ten years to create happiness.'

It sounds like a jail sentence. 'Only then can you claim to become the true married couple.' She's still looking down in her lap as he goes on to describe his wife's misery in early marriage.

'Your mother wasn't happy at the start . . . We had our troubles for years . . . I found her weeping in the kitchen so many times. But your mother put up with me. You must have faith, and love one another. Show Satake all the warm affection you've shown me. OK? Then the true, new happiness will emerge.'

Noriko looks crushed under this onslaught of solemn chivvying. 'Understand?'

She nods, slowly, deeply, impassively.

'You understand, don't you?'

'Yes. Sorry for being so selfish.'

'So you understood me.'

'Yes . . . I was very selfish.'

'I'm glad you understood me. I didn't want you to marry feeling the way you did.' Whereas now at least she knows she's not expected to enjoy it.

'Marry him. I'm sure you'll be happy. It's not difficult.'

'Yes.'

'I'm sure you'll make a great couple. I'm looking forward to it. Soon we'll laugh about this talk we're having tonight.' If not in two years, then perhaps in ten.

She says, 'I'm sorry . . .' again, and looks up at him as she goes on, '. . . for worrying you all the time.'

'So . . . be happy. OK?'

'Yes. I will surely be happy.'

'Yes. I'm sure you will. I know you can do it.' His assertion becomes less convincing with every repetition.

'I'm very confident. Be happy.'

'Yes.'

She turns back to her suitcase and carries on packing.

Somehow this whole scene escapes notice in the shadow of the mighty Zen vase. I don't mind celebrated critics like Paul Schrader and Donald Richie seeing tearfulness where there isn't any, but I do mind their being so mesmerised by ceramics and the resignation so mysteriously expressed by such objects that they don't notice Noriko making one last desperate bid to avoid her marriage. The vase shot doesn't dominate the film, but it seems to dominate discussions of it, looming over the skyline of its aesthetics.

I don't pretend to be an expert in Japanese family structure, but I can't help feeling that what Noriko is proposing for herself (staying on in her father's household after his remarriage) is a humiliating de-motion. All the freedom of her life, as conveyed in the first forty minutes of the film, would evaporate with someone else in charge. Her unmarried status, which up to this point has had the flavour of virt-uous sacrifice, would be indistinguishable in the altered circumstances from failure. She would lose all her old privileges without gaining any new ones, in the way that she would if she became a wife.

The mystery of Noriko's profound flinching from marriage is raised all over again by her pleading to be allowed to occupy this dim niche of family life, The Daughter Who Has Nowhere Else To Go. In her conversation with Aya she imagined earning her own living, a role that calls for skills, and an assertiveness, that are clearly beyond her. Now she contemplates an equally drastic move in the opposite direction, staying where she is but suppressing the wholeness of her personality. Any course of action, however impractical, has more appeal to her than the one mandated by 'humans and history'.

Her father slowly extinguishes this last hope with his litany of undermining reassurances. She looks down at her lap as his homily stumbles on, bowing her head in an acquiescence which is no more than a form of despair. If tears are useful indicators of emotional states, as the Western tradition assumes, then it's worth pointing out that this is the scene (rather than the vase passage) in which Noriko discreetly wipes a tear away, her face half-crumpling – it's at 1:36:28 – between her father saying 'I know you can do it' and 'I'm confident.'

By this stage of the film, audiences are likely to be so habituated to the convention of a pillow shot that a standard unmeditative cut to a different scene produces an effect of shock. The next scene is different in geography, chronology and atmosphere.

We see a large and formal car parked outside a house. There are three boys in caps sitting on steps or on the pavement, while a larger boy in a sailor cap bounces a ball against a wall. Then he climbs onto the car's running board and bounces up and down there, rocking the car on its suspension. He reaches in to sound the horn. He rocks again and sounds the horn again, a soft double blast.

The note of the horn almost seems to form part of the music, which paraphrases 'Here Comes the Bride' without subtlety.

We're back in the family's home town of Kamakura and Noriko has been busy, as of course has Aunt Masa. It's Noriko's wedding day, but we've skipped over the intimate preparations so as to rejoin the narrative just before the bride disappears into her ritual role.

Inside the house, the professor and Hattori are smoking side by side in cane chairs. The professor has been reunited with his cigarette holder.

Hattori says, 'I worried when it drizzled last night', as 'Here Comes the Bride' plays relentlessly on.

The professor turns towards him with a smile. 'Yes. I'm glad it cleared up. Rain makes things difficult.'

'It does.'

Of course sometimes, when people talk about the weather, in Britain or Japan, they are doing no more than that, but their comments might also refer to Noriko's personal meteorology. If she was crying the night before then it is indeed a good thing that she has stopped. Tears on a wedding day do make things difficult, if they're the wrong kind of tears (like that 'wrong kind of snow' which brings disruption to British trains). Am I being sucked into the vortex of over-interpretation? Occupational disease of the critic. It gets so many of the best of us in the end. The bends, the bends! Our lungs fill up with insight and we drown.

The professor turns to Hattori with a suggestion of suddenness, as if he's just thought of something. 'Where did you go on your honeymoon?'

'Yugawara.'

'Noriko's going there, too. Are there only buses from the station?'

There's an abrupt change of shot at this point, so that we see the two of them from the other side. This breaks Hollywood continuity but is perfectly lucid. We mentally assemble the perspectives without conscious effort. The price of coherence is constant, subliminal vigilance, and we pay it all the time.

'No,' says Hattori, 'you can get a taxi.'

'Oh, there are taxis?'

'Yes.'

The housekeeper comes in now. Yes, she's

come out of her box for this special occasion. This scene corroborates her existence in some sense, but without really clarifying what's going on. Her presence isn't remotely mysterious here – no one would expect standard arrangements on this day of all days. There are two dressers upstairs attending to Noriko, after all, but it would be silly to imagine that they had ever put in an appearance before. Still, it's good to know she isn't actually a hallucination, an emanation of the empty house which rises up to receive visitors and do odd mending jobs. She's unlikely to be a ghost, like the wife who serves her husband food and drink near the end of *Ogetsu Monogatari*.

The presence of the 'housekeeper' in this scene wouldn't draw any attention to itself, with audiences thinking 'who can that woman possibly be?', if it wasn't for her earlier appearance. That's the disconcerting moment (though in practice audiences pay no attention), the moment when she accepts the thank-you present and wedding photograph from Hattori on behalf of the absent family members.

The woman, whoever she is, says the professor is wanted upstairs. Noriko is ready to be seen, she says, and such a beautiful bride . . .

As the professor approaches the bottom of the stairs Masa almost falls down them in her hurry and excitement. 'Oh, she's ready now.'

'I see.'

'Is the car ready?'

'It's outside.'

'Good.' Masa turns round and heads up the stairs again, anxious to show off what she presumably thinks of as her handiwork.

Noriko is sitting in finery, with two attendants behind her, her head cast down. There's no animation in her face, though the tassels of the costume swing a little.

The professor thanks one of the attendants.

'All ready, eh?' he says.

Noriko looks up and gives a smile, but now the camera shows her from the opposite side, skewing the perspectives. If the people are assumed not to have changed their positions, then she isn't looking at him or anywhere near him. As experienced audiences we mentally push the images towards convergence, but it takes a certain amount of effort to reconcile the points of view.

Noriko's father nods appreciatively several times. She nods wanly back. The shot of her nodding shows her reflected in a mirror – in other words, their gazes have been meeting in a mirror all along, but it is only now that we are given the information. This is a sort of double bluff on Ozu's part. He only appeared to be breaking the rules of film language. If we had been shown the mirror earlier in the sequence there would have been no mystery, and no moment to make us experience separation rather than sharing. The sense of discrepancy, of things not quite adding up, not yielding a tidy meaning, is strong in the film, and in this sequence. When the eye lines don't match up, there can be no agreement about reality.

The lead attendant says, 'We'll go ahead.'

'Thank you.'

The other one says, 'I'll take this,' 'this' being some sort of cushion or embroidered bag. Now it's just the family, and Noriko's head sinks again. First Masa and then the professor take up position on the floor.

The next shot of Noriko is from a different angle. Her eyes are in shadow. Her head sinks further from the horizontal.

Aunt Masa asks, 'Nori-chan, do you have your fan?' The use of a pet name can be a way of keeping a junior or weaker person in her place.

'Yes,' Noriko says, reaching up to her sash. Unless this is just a fidget, she is identifying where the fan is tucked.

'You're such a beautiful bride,' Masa goes on. 'I wish your mother could see you.' See you, that is, on the threshold of the pilgrimage of tears that is marriage as she experienced it. Aunt Masa's face distorts and she leans forward, wiping away a tear.

Her brother doesn't join in the emotional display, though as the widower he would seem to be more closely involved than a sister-in-law. He puts out his cigarette in an ashtray by his side and says, 'Well, shall we be going? We don't want to be rushed.'

'Do you have anything to say to her?' says Masa.

'No, I have nothing more to say.' This sounds rather discouraging, though considering the number of false notes he struck the last time he gave a lecture on marriage his silence can be counted a blessing.

'Then, Nori-chan, let's go.'

Noriko nods under her headdress. Masa bows as she gets up, then adjusts the fall of Noriko's costume.

The music plays its indefatigable 'Amazing Grace' theme, but with the minor interval associated with Noriko's first unhappiness when she learned of the plans being made around her.

Noriko kneels, arranging her costume carefully, and addresses the professor. 'Father . . .'

Her head sinks, and though the professor goes down on his haunches to be more on a level with her, the headdress makes most of her face invisible. She looks up at him, with no trace of a smile.

'These many long years . . .' she begins and then bites her lip, as if overcome by her feelings. She continues illogically, as if she was unable to finish a prepared speech, '. . . thank you for everything.' Her head sinks again during these words, so that she is now presenting the top of her head-dress to her father rather than any part of her face or person.

Of course it's traditional across cultures for a

wedding dress to be restricting. The bride becomes a ritual object in her own right. It wouldn't be much of a wedding dress if it could serve for other occasions, worn to bake a cake or run for a bus. The whole point of a wedding dress is that it should disqualify the wearer from any activity except getting married. Obviously it makes a difference whether getting married is in fact something you want to do. Not every caterpillar wants to pupate. Some would rather stay put on the self-renewing nibbled leaf that has always been their home.

Noriko's vitality is dimmed rather than enhanced by her costume and regalia. If this is the feeling-tone of 'late spring', what will autumn and winter be like? She goes to her wedding as if to her grave.

Her father's smile is constant in this scene, not fixed in a way that suggests falseness but unvaryingly attuned to a mood at odds with Noriko's. 'Be happy,' he says, 'and be a good wife.'

'I will,' she says, her face still entirely replaced by the swathing of her headdress.

'Be happy,' he says again. The chrysalis in front of him nods in obedient misery. She raises her head to him. Again he says, 'Remember, be a good wife,' and she says, 'Yes, I will.' Her expression is close to ghastly at this point, with the trademark smile superimposed on eyes that shine with loss. Her head sinks again under the weight of her headdress, or its implications. The music is throughly sombre, with all of the 'Here Comes the Bride' bounce gone out of it.

Her father smiles on. 'Shall we go?' he says.

The shot changes, to show Noriko kneeling between her father and aunt. She is turned away from the camera. The professor helps her rise to her feet, and she walks from the room, still turned away from us. Masa follows carrying a suitcase and a bag. Then she stops, turns round and does a vigilant little circuit of the room. It's not anything as unseemly as a lap of honour, though she might feel entitled to one after making the wedding happen, shoehorning the recalcitrant grub into its ceremonial cocoon at long last. She's just making sure Noriko hasn't forgotten anything.

This is her finest, tenderest moment in the film, the only time she is genuinely mindful of the needs of another. We're being shown a quite new side of her. When she's all alone in the room Masa can be remarkably considerate.

The camera dwells for a few seconds on the empty space she has left. Then we're back in the street outside. The boy playing on the car (Bu-chan, if that's him) joins a scrum of children pressing to get a glimpse of the (unseen) wedding party. Others scurry past the camera to join them. Some climb on the rear bumper of the car for a better view.

They may be able to see the wedding party, but we can't. This could almost be a prophetic out-take from Buñuel's *Exterminating Angel* (1963), in which guests are unable to leave a party when an invisible barrier intervenes.

As far as the viewer's experience goes, Noriko has already taken her leave of the film. She's gone. We don't see her again. The same is true of Aunt Masa, though her absence from the film after this point is less surprising. Her final little circuit of the room upstairs could be understood as a sort of curtain call, soliciting the conflicted applause that is her entitlement.

In effect Noriko left earlier, when she withheld her face, first from her father and then from the camera, towards the end of the last scene. You could say that she left long before that, in the sense that the carefree personality which seemed to be her essence only flickeringly survived the midpoint of the film. Her smile made a few comebacks, but the ease it had seemed to embody had gone for good.

Her body language is inhibited in the second half of the film even before she submits to the further restriction of wedding costume. Compare the earlier expressiveness she showed with Aya, the flexibility of her shoulders at a moment of fond teasing (41:10), or her lightness of foot at 43:35, when she all but skipped across the room at Masa's house before the auntly bombshell was dropped on her blitheness.

Just the same, it's an extraordinary decision on

Ozu's part not to follow Noriko any further than he does. We see a woman prepare for the central rite of passage in her life, but we don't see her go through with it. We don't even see her leave the house. From our point of view the ritual is botched because incomplete, however it turns out for her. An interrupted ceremony makes a happy or unhappy marriage equally impossible, and we're left with a sense of something prematurely broken off, defective, invalidated.

The next shot shows, for a good few seconds, the window and mirror in the room that Noriko has just left. There follows a longer shot, lasting nearly ten seconds, of the whole room. Audiences seeing the film for the first time have no reason to think that they won't be seeing the wedding itself, but even so the effect of a premature mourning is strong. The room might belong to someone who has died, like the rooms at the end of *The Dam Busters*, the rooms of airmen who will not return to them. Even before it becomes clear that we haven't been invited to witness the wedding ceremony, the emphasis is firmly on loss and absence. It's a fetishisation of the immediate past, the past before it is cold, and represents a peculiar entrapped state of mind, as if there was no future life to be lived.

Cut to Professor Somiya and Aya at the bar in a restaurant, a place (the Takigawa) familiar from earlier in the film. It's where the theme of sexual disgust, now dying enigmatically away, was first sounded. He's still smart in his morning coat and wing collar, pouring himself some *sake*. She plays with the carnation she's holding, and helps herself to some snack or other from a dish out of our sight.

The professor addresses her with a diminutive form of her name and offers some *sake*: 'Aya-chan, do you want some?' Perhaps it's only Masa's diminutives which express a desire for control. Aya picks up her cup, which was also out of sight, knocks it back, and holds it out for a refill. In the previous scene at this address Noriko, a more old-fashioned sort of girl, poured out for Onodera but didn't take a drink herself.

'This is my third,' Aya says with quiet pride. Professor Somiya produces one of the non-committal noises from his wide selection.

'I can handle five,' she goes on. Aya has learned to boast about her capacity, one more Western habit among so many.

'Once I drank six,' she says, 'and I fell down.'

'Did you?' He doesn't seem shocked.

The bartender puts down two bowls of food in front of them, remarking that Onodera and Noriko visited the bar recently.

'I've heard that,' says the professor.

The bartender claims to have been amazed – she was so grown up. 'She's not with you today?'

He explains that he and Aya just saw her off at Tokyo station, after her wedding.

'Did she? And you saw her off? Many congratulations.' He bows.

'Thank you.'

The bartender addresses a few words to a departing customer and moves out of shot. Aya, on her third *sake*, is in a mood to be direct. 'Uncle!' she calls out. She returns the favour he performed a few moments ago by filling his cup from the flask of *sake*. It's as if the thought of Noriko has improved her manners.

Aya smiles dreamily, saying 'Where would she be now?'

'Oh, I would say around Ofuna.' There's a faint noise of rolling stock on the soundtrack, either lending atmosphere to the discussion of Noriko's train journey or there to suggest it in the first place.

'Probably. You'll be lonely from now on.' Aya doesn't wrap things up, does she?

A further non-committal noise. 'Not too much,' he says. 'I'll get used to it.' He picks up the *sake* flask and asks if Aya is ready for her fourth. Technically she's not, since there's still some left in her cup, but she knocks it back very willingly.

For the first time Professor Somiya looks a bit blank, and Aya says again, 'Uncle . . .'

Her look is suddenly softer as she asks, 'Are you really going to remarry?'

He perks up a bit and asks, 'Why?'

Aya's manner is poised between flirting and

scolding as she says, 'It worried Noriko. That seemed to bother her the most.'

He makes no comment.

Aya goes on, 'Don't do it. Why would you do it again? You mustn't.' She seems to have reached the end of her enthusiasm for marriage as a state to be urged on all comers. 'Okay?'

He smiles, which she takes for agreement.

'Really?' she asks.

He makes a noise that is by his standards unambiguously affirmative. 'But if I had said otherwise she wouldn't have married.'

She leans over suddenly and kisses his forehead. He looks baffled. What has he done to deserve it?

'You're wonderful,' she says. 'Terrific. I'm impressed.' She's laughing, apparently delighted by what he has said. 'Don't worry,' she goes on, 'You won't be lonely. I'll visit you often. Really.'

He nods. 'Yes. Please do, Aya-chan.'

'I certainly will. I feel wonderful.' As she says so, she pats her cheeks with her hands. It's the *sake*, presumably, which is warming her mood so strongly. She finishes her cup and holds it out, saying brazenly 'Now, I'll take my fifth.' He pours it for her. She knocks it back in one, then turns the cup upside down, saying firmly, 'The end.' She looks over at him.

'Remember,' he says, 'I'll be expecting you. Please come.'

'Of course,' she says. 'I promised. I don't tell lies like you do.'

He asks what she means.

She laughs. 'Or not so convincingly.'

This is the point where I take Aya to have some slight moral authority. For all her flightiness she hasn't abandoned honourable standards of conduct, while the professor has tricked Noriko into leaving home.

Oh dear, I hope I haven't destroyed Aya's integrity (now that I need to call on it) by speculating that she might be claiming credit for baking that was actually done by the hired help . . .

The professor laughs quite harshly in his turn. 'It couldn't be helped,' he says. 'It was the biggest lie of my life.'

She tops up his cup and looks at him fondly, making some sort of chewing motion which Aunt Masa would certainly find vulgar.

The closing passages of the film are low-key, but there is a certain abruptness about them also. The 'pillow shots' which seemed so much a part of the rhythm and texture of the film, those moments of repose, have dropped away. Pillow shots produce an effect of stasis but are part of the dynamism of the film. They gave an impression of serenity that was unwarranted, or was withdrawn as the film went on. The contrasts between sequences are no longer softened as they were, and repose has gone by the board. Pillow shots are either absent or call attention to themselves self-defeatingly – the odd series of Zen-garden shots in the Kyoto section can hardly perform a pillow function, when the element of otherness, of radiant indifference, is complicated by such emphatic use of film language.

Call them *mu* shots instead, as some do, nothingness shots, and the paradox is even more striking. Why is there less of this anchoring nothingness towards the end of the film?

Now, between the end of the restaurant scene with Aya and the professor returning home, there is a shot of the interior of the Takigawa, where they have been. Now the space is deserted. We see it first with the lights on and then in darkness. Although the shot is empty, it isn't an 'empty shot' but has a narrative implication. What it implies is that the professor has stayed until chucking-out time. He's in no hurry to go home. What is there for him to return to?

We see him on the last leg of the journey home, still in his wedding finery, weaving a little. Perhaps he's not as hard-headed as Aya when it comes to *sake* consumption. He's smoking a cigarette, which he throws away before entering the house.

As he enters, a woman comes out of the sitting room and greets him. She doesn't show her face, but she's clearly the anomalous housekeeper. She offers her congratulations on the wedding. He thanks her, and she leaves. They exchange 'good nights'. He asks her to pass on his regards to 'Sei', presumably the husband who was doing yardwork in the earlier scene.

This pretty much clears up the servant question. Not only does this person not live on the premises, she doesn't offer to do anything for him, as a servant would. He has to hang up his coat himself. She can only be a neighbour who has been tidying up after the wedding, perhaps keeping an eye on the house.

It's odd, all the same, that she doesn't offer to keep the professor company, doesn't fuss over him even to the extent of a cup of tea. Having her leave immediately seems to ride the loneliness theme rather hard. In discussing his future, admittedly, whether with Noriko or Aya, and painting as rosy a picture as he can, the professor makes no mention of neighbours as a source of company. If these do odd jobs for him then perhaps their social standing is lower than his own, but loneliness need not accept such restrictions.

In fact there's a reference to 'Sei' much earlier in the film. When Noriko comes home and a game of mah-jong is on the cards (or the tiles), the professor asks 'Is Sei in?' This is before Noriko vetoes the game on the grounds that there is still work to be done. So Sei is a neighbour who sometimes makes the necessary fourth at mah-jong. Possibly when the professor and Noriko are on their own Sei's wife makes up the numbers, but there's no sign of any resulting social closeness in the scene after Noriko's wedding.

Do I make too much of the servant theme? I'm standing my ground. The whole film boils down to the question: who belongs in this household? Noriko seems to fit her surroundings perfectly, but she has to go.

And to me the earlier scene remains mysterious. Most of the ambiguity could have been cleared up with a single line of a dialogue when Hattori appears ('I live next door – just popped in to do some darning.'), though even so she seems to be making herself rather too much at home.

One possibility, risking the bends again, is that the conventions have been reversed. In other words, it isn't the scene when Hattori leaves the wedding photograph that violates realism, it's all the other ones at the house, and this scene (with father and daughter absent) has been left at odds with the rest as a marker of what has been changed elsewhere.

I don't know in demographic terms whether a professor sharing a house with his daughter in 1949 would have staff of some sort. Doesn't it seem likely? After all, Aya has domestic help for such arduous tasks as cake transport. Even in a decadent Americanised post-war world it's hardly likely that a stenographer would earn more than a university professor, or have a higher status to live up to.

In that case, Ozu has stylised the domestic scenes

of *Late Spring* by removing the real-life presence of help in such a household from the refracted world of the film. In real life Noriko would not warm the *sake*, nor the professor run his own bath – let alone concern himself with the temperature of bathwater pleasing to his daughter. In the film they do. The effect, of course, would be to create a tone of intense intimacy, with father and daughter meeting each other's needs with a glowing undemonstrative consideration. Very much the quality which has given *Late Spring* its unique atmosphere and prestige.

Left alone in the house, the professor looks around the room, and brushes fluff off the sleeves of his jacket, a residual Noriko-gesture he seems to have taken on. Then he takes the jacket off and puts it on a hanger. No question of dropping it on the floor, now that there's no longer anyone to pick it up.

He sits down on the cane chair he was occupying earlier on, when he was discussing the weather of the wedding with Hattori. The camera angle changes as he sits, so that a group of apples is prominent at the left of the shot.

There is a bowl of apples similarly visible in the first scene, the one of the tea ceremony, if we need to be reminded that Ozu plans his effects.

He gives a sigh, then reaches for the nearest apple and a knife, starting to pare it so as to keep the peel in a single spiral, making sure the blade is conveniently positioned by turning the fruit in his left hand. We switch over to the other side to monitor this delicate, matter-of-fact operation.

The camera shows his face as he concentrates on the task in hand. The noise of what he's doing sounds surprisingly scratchy on the soundtrack. A close-up of the apple shows that he has peeled it right to the end. He severs the last edge and the spiral of peel falls to the floor.

He bows his head, as Noriko bowed her head to him earlier in the day, with the same acquiescence in despair. He lets his arms relax so that the apple and the knife are no longer in shot.

Then the film reaches its end with a shot, lasting twenty seconds, of the sea at night.

All in all rather a downbeat finale. It's not surprising that the film's internet fan base should have some rather pumped-up readings of the professor's last scene. One person thought he was so drunk as to be falling into a stupor, another that he died before our eyes.

Nothing so overdone. What we are shown is only a small death of the will to live, to keep going. When he starts his peeling he presumably has some faint desire for the fruit, but by the time it is ready to eat he has lost interest. He has put in the effort of preparing it but the little reward he has worked for means nothing to him. His sense of purpose has fallen away in the time it takes to peel an apple.

The final shot of the sea is desolate or comforting according to taste. Most viewers take it to correspond in some way with the professor's state of mind, if only to chasten it with the indifference of the cosmos. How many viewers of the film remember that it's another character who is associated with the sea? In his discussion of local landmarks with Onodera the professor described the seaside as being fifteen minutes away, but it's Noriko who goes there on her bicycling expedition with Hattori, on a day of sunshine and possibility. It makes just as much sense to treat it as the end-point of the Noriko strand, with the sparkle of her day at the seaside giving way to a dark vista of cowed little waves.

It seems fair to say that *Late Spring* is a slippery work of art, even when it's not being deliberately deceptive. Take that apple, for instance, in the last scene, that apple so saturated with pathos. Is it even an apple? Japanese culture prefers red apples, and yes, I have noticed that the film is in black and white, but it looks paler than you would expect from a red one. It's more likely to be a sand pear, fruit of the tree *Pyrus pyrifolia*, also known as the *nashi* pear, structurally very similar to the apple. Something of a luxury item, often served to guests or given as gifts. The tree symbolises spring in many parts of East Asia, but its fruit of course represents autumn. *Nashi* may be used as an autumn *kigo*, or 'season word', when writing haiku. Do I know what that means? Not really. But I do know that there is an element of elusiveness in the film, which may be a key component of its durability.

Even the most basic precis of the story seems to go wrong. Belatedly I notice that this is how *Late Spring* is summed up on the packaging of the Tartan DVD I've been watching so closely: 'the exquisite and moving tale of . . . a young woman who sacrifices her independence to dedicate herself to her ailing father'. Fairer to say that her independence co-exists very happily with her care for her father. It's only threatened by the marriage she resists so hard. And there's nothing in the film about his being 'ailing', unless you count the use of a stick which doubles as a natty accessory. Noriko is the one with the hospital appointment and the history of poor health. Although she has officially recovered from whatever illness she suffered, a number of people in the film ask her if she's tired, not just her father but also Hattori and Onodera, as if exhaustion had been a recognised part of her life to date.

One of the things that makes Japanese culture seem hermetic is the way the language is written. You couldn't be much of an authority on France without being able to read French, even on Russia without being able to read Russian, but you can be drenched in Japanese culture without being able to read the characters in which the language is written down. That's the case, for instance, with Donald Richie.

So a Westerner who is able to read Japanese has the huge advantage of having access to the documentary record. Lars-Martin Sorensen is one of this small crew, and a book of his published by the Edwin Mellen Press in 2009 is of huge interest. Unfortunately the linguistic advantage isn't enough to make him a particularly sharp critic. In fact his interpretations are often nutty – he's like an explorer who comes back with a rich collection of specimens jumbled in cardboard boxes, gorgeous beaks and strangely articulated feet sticking out of them, but has no idea how to classify them. Nevertheless his book enriches many of the mysteries of *Late Spring* with its brute research value.

Edwin Mellen Press has had a very patchy reputation on the internet over the last decade, as if it was closer to a vanity imprint, what with tiny print runs and exorbitant cover price, than a respectable academic publisher. I've seen it said that you should go with any other publisher if you have a choice, from the point of view of your resumé – but Sorenson's book offers a couple of bursts of dazzling illumination, along with some damp squibs and several arguments that fizzle.

His title is *Censorship of Japanese Films During the U.S. Occupation of Japan*. That's right, censorship. It's not exactly a secret, just something that people keep on forgetting to mention.

Anderson and Richie's *The Japanese Film* goes

into a certain amount of detail about the constraints on film production. Censorship wasn't a constant force – films that were passed without objection in 1946 would have had a hard time being made a couple of years later. But though it was inconsistent it wasn't optional. It was still something that had to be dealt with.

Perhaps the subject makes criticism squeamish because the idea of politically dictated or prohibited subject matter threatens the autonomy of the director. How could films made under such restrictions represent one person's artistic vision?

This may be setting the bar too high. Film is a medium both collaborative and expensive, and it's rare even under the most favourable circumstances for a film to bear a single fingerprint. Ozu himself didn't necessarily see people in his position as rulers of their own little worlds, and he had a beguiling description of his own dependence on the marketplace: 'After all, film directors are like prostitutes under a bridge, hiding their faces and calling out to customers.'

Hiding their faces, perhaps, because what you get, even in the most reductive transaction, need not be what you bargained for.

Style is at least as strong a consideration as subject-matter. Formalism insists that an artist needn't start with personal meanings, but has no alternative but to end with them. There's an analogy here with free association in Freudian analysis. When it was first proposed that analysands should say whatever came into their minds, it was objected that the word-stream could easily be faked, but that isn't actually a problem, since the same conflicts are in evidence either way. We can't determine our meanings, but nor can we avoid them however hard we try. The David Lynch who made *The Straight Story* for Disney in 1999, from a script not his own, produced something that was unmistakably continuous with his cinematic world, though lacking sex, violence and other trademarks.

It doesn't matter to me, as a viewer of *Late Spring*, that the director himself never married but lived with his mother. It doesn't matter to me that he was expelled from school at one point for writing a love letter to another boy, though this seems very important to Robin Wood, a fascinating critic who came out as gay, relatively late in life, and tried to bring as many of his favourite directors with him as he could, some of them blinking with confusion in the light he shone on them.

It does matter to me that an expert film-maker negotiated institutional requirements, not because this invalidates the resulting film but because it demonstrates that obstacles can be turned to advantage. There is no better school of subtlety than censorship.

Ozu's two films before *Late Spring* (*Record*

*of a Tenement Gentleman* and *Hen in the Wind*) were relatively raw in their treatment of war damage, both physical and social, but censorship was no longer so accommodating by the time he made *Late Spring*. There was concern on the part of the forces of occupation that Japanese culture was not properly responding to the new democratic values imposed on it.

Period films had always been discouraged by the censors, for fear of promoting feudal values, though Mizoguchi got a dispensation (for *Utamaro*) as early as 1946. Now there was increasing pressure brought to bear on film-makers not to endorse traditional marriage customs.

*Late Spring* is the template for late Ozu, but its turning away from broader social issues, its preoccupation with family life, were not necessarily free choices. Luckily in art a choice doesn't have to be free to be rich.

So the vein of *Late Spring* was a rewarding one, even if not freely chosen. Ozu had collaborated with Kogo Noda before the war, but this was the first time since then that they had worked together. Is that significant? Were they a good smuggling partnership, when it came to running contraband meanings past customs? Ozu never worked without him again.

Because the two films before *Late Spring* aren't so well known, and the films that follow are so continuous with its manner, no one remarks on the discontinuity that this particular film represents. It's a hinge so well oiled that critics tend not to notice Ozu's world pivoting into a new phase.

In fact the censors had no major objections to the story of *Late Spring* but wanted 'the feudalistic family relations of old Japan' to be presented as undesirable in a democratic country. There's irony aplenty in the idea that democratic principles must be autocratically imposed, but censors are not attuned to that wavelength.

They seem to have mistaken *Late Spring* for a tale of arranged marriage. It was hardly a subject on which they were likely to be experts. Censorship is a set of rules, not a system of thought. They may not have noticed that there is indeed an arranged marriage in the film, but it's not the one at the centre of the film. It's the one between Noriko's parents, the one which led to years of kitchen weeping before an accommodation was reached. That's one more reason for the professor's speech deserving every all-time-worst pep-talk award going. He's not comparing like with like – why should Noriko, exercising freedom of choice in an utterly different world, have a future with tears built into it as a necessary ingredient?

In the script submitted to the censors, the visit to Kyoto included a visit to the mother's grave. This was suspect under the new rules, as an indication of retrogressive religious practice – though if visiting a parent's grave counts as ancestor worship, then there's a lot of it about. Secret Shinto pops up in the most surprising places.

It was also to have been made clear, originally, that Noriko's parents had once spent time at the inn where father and daughter choose to stay. These details would have made a contribution to the wholeness of the family portrait, but their absence is hardly crucial.

The censors were bothered by Aunt Masa's light fingers on the wallet she finds, and stipulated that she should surrender it to the authorities. Ozu both obeyed and disobeyed this directive, by having the responsible citizen's course of action clearly described and indefinitely deferred. Clearly there was an element of play involved. What goes on between the censor and the censored is a sort of dance, a *danse macabre* at worst, but it can be something more courtly, a pavane of sly feinting, deceptive deference. It's easy to see that Yasujiro Ozu knew the steps and was light on his feet.

In principle there was a hefty jail sentence in store for anyone who broke the rules. Sorenson doesn't state whether this penalty was ever invoked – if any such proceedings were public the image of the occupiers would suffer, and there would be a risk of making martyrs. Any mention of censorship in the press was itself censored, so in theory Japanese readers and viewers had no idea that the world around them was passing through any number of sieves and filters before it reached the newspaper page or the cinema screen.

It seems more likely that the usual penalties for non-compliance were financial and indirect. Erosion of revenue is at least as powerful a deterrent as legal sanction. Film-makers who infringed the rules were required to re-edit, and if necessary to shoot new footage, to ensure that the public was presented with a seamless artefact. Such adjustments don't come cheap.

Delay itself is a penalty. One Kurosawa film, *Desertion at Dawn* (1950) was rewritten seven times before the censors passed it. The whole process took two years.

The mechanism for censorship set up by SCAP (Supreme Commander Allied Powers) was somewhat bureaucratic, though it was certainly intended to function more efficiently than it did in the case of *Desertion at Dawn*. Film-makers were required to submit a synopsis for approval first. Objectionable material could be removed at an early stage, before money had been committed.

There were two separate agencies responsible for different aspects of censorship: the Civil Information and Education section of SCAP and the Civil Censorship Detachment. CI&E was charged with the diffusion of positive propaganda, CCD with removing negative themes and images. First a synopsis was submitted to CI&E. A week or so after submission there would be a conference between staff and the film-makers. If the synopsis was approved, then a script could be submitted. CI&E would offer recommendations and suggestions.

Then the script would be passed to CCD. The provisionally finished film would be screened to the CI&E censors, then passed on with their comments to CCD, who would have their own screening. Any objectionable material would be deleted at this stage. Instructions might be given for further adjustments (re-editing, re-shooting). Finally the CCD gave the film its stamp of approval – without which no cinema was allowed to screen it.

Both agencies, CI&E and CCD, were understaffed. There was much more work than had been anticipated when they were originally set up. Even so, they managed to squabble over their duties. By March 1946 CCD was complaining about CI&E exceeding its powers, making decisions about what should be cut when its role was supposed to be the shaping of positive portrayals of the newly democratised Japan. CCD was largely staffed by army personnel, CI&E by civilians, yet it was the civilian body which took the harder line on certain subjects. A film's choice of the sword as a weapon might have a feudal and militaristic implication, but CCD was able to see that that the context of the action was important. It wasn't simply that the sword was a taboo object.

Sometimes a film which had already been passed gave offence in an unexpected quarter. A film from 1946 called *The Japanese Tragedy* was banned on the orders of General Willoughby after the Japanese prime minister complained, although the censors had found nothing objectionable about it. Understandably, the exemplary financial setback of having to withdraw a film at the last moment made the industry in general more cautious in its choice of subject matter. One of the first and most obvious consequences of censorship is timidity, self-censorship, a turning away from confrontation. Japanese newspapers rapidly learned how to keep out of trouble. A law can be an effective agent of repression without ever leading to a court case.

It's easy to show that by the time of *Late Spring* (synopsis and script submitted on 12 April and 5 May respectively, conference held on 13 May) the censors were objecting to things which they had been happy to wave through a few years before. In the script, Onodera had a bit of dialogue about the statue of Takamori Saigo in Ueno Park. The specific reference had to be removed. Saigo (1828–77) was an opponent of Westernisation in his day, and might now function as a possible rallying point for nationalistic sentiment.

In the finished film, Onodera reminds Noriko that they saw a boy shooting at a pigeon on an unspecified statue in the park, 'just like William Tell'. The BFI's subtitles render this as 'just like William Hart', which is indeed the name that Onodera seems to be saying, though the reference becomes nonsensical.

Yet the last scene of *Record of a Tenement Gentleman* had shown the same statue without ruffling any occupation feathers. It's true that it wasn't referred to by name, but if the script of *Late Spring* is any guide (the script of *Record of a Tenement Gentleman* seems not to have been preserved) locations had to be specified. The ragged children who surround the statue in the film, orphaned or abandoned, smoking and scratching themselves, offer by their very presence a harsher view of the post-war world than the authorities wanted to promote, but there seems to have been more leeway in 1947 than 1949.

Sorenson even wonders if bribery might have played a part in the passing of *Record of a Tenement Gentleman*. It seems odd to him that a film should feature the traditional neighbourhood associations in the very year they were banned by the authorities. The only evidence he can produce is that a CI&E censor called Clifford Toshio Konno objected to the theme of the mistreatment of children. He was later given a dishonourable discharge on unspecified grounds. Those troubling sequences were then passed by another *nisei*-censor (a *nisei* being a first-generation Japanese-American) called George Ishikawa.

I suppose it's a possibility, though the logic isn't

clear to me. If Konno is supposed to have been on the take, bribed to nod through subversive material, what was he doing objecting to things in the film?

It may just have been that an increasingly sophisticated awareness of Japanese culture made the censors realise that Saigo could be seen as a figurehead by retrograde elements in society. In the script of *Late Spring*, reference to 'Lord Yoritomo' was made less specific ('feudal lords'), presumably because of a similar sensitivity. Yoritomo forced the Emperor to proclaim him 'commander-in-chief against the barbarians' (the barbarians at the time being the indigenous Ainu).

The occupying forces would typically have had only a three-month crash course in Japanese language and culture, but perhaps nuances could be learned on the job. (There was also a growing number of Japanese nationals working as censors, but that has to count as an ambiguous factor.)

There are other examples of changing standards. In one of the Kyoto scenes in the original script for *Late Spring* the professor says, 'There is no place like this in Tokyo.' The script submitted for approval by the censors then gives him the fragmentary sentence 'All the ruined . . .'

In 1949 this was not permissible. The word 'ruined' was marked for deletion, and Ozu substituted the word 'dusty'. Dust was permitted but ruination was not to be spoken of. Yet in *A Certain*

*Night's Kiss*, back in 1946, though there was coyness about the meeting of lips promised by the title, there was frankness about war damage, and the lovers walked not through back-projected rose gardens but charred terrain.

The curious thing is that the system of censorship was changing just when *Late Spring* was being vetted. The following month, June 1949, when the film was actually in production, responsibility for censorship was transferred to a new body, the Japanese 'Film Ethics Regulation Control Committee'. Completed films needed clearance from the CI&E right up to April 1952 and the end of the occupation, but even so it looks as if, at the relevant moment, the system of control set up by the forces of occupation was simultaneously cracking down and falling apart.

Sorenson's thesis is that Ozu was throughly opposed to Western ways, but that censorship prevented him from saying so. Instead he sent coded messages about the superiority of the past.

He produces evidence of various strengths and flavours to support his position. Contemporary Japanese reviews of *Late Spring* described is as pure and wholesome, a world away from the problems of the modern world. Sometimes this was a compliment, sometimes a criticism. Fair enough, as far as it goes. Then Sorenson analyses the composition of the post-war cinema audience in Japan, establishing that it was mainly young and had therefore had its values formed in the militaristic culture that ended so abruptly in 1945. Again, fair enough. Then he proposes that Ozu uses place names, historic capitals, in the film to convey his meaning.

Noriko and her father live in Kamakura, where the samurai caste founded its first *bakufu* ('tent government') in 1192. Important scenes take place in Tokyo, that parvenu of cities, which only became the capital in 1868. Father and daughter make their last trip together to Kyoto, capital from 794 to 1185. The only city missing from the set is Nara, the imperial capital from about 645 to 794, and that's because the censors discouraged what they took to be a theme of ancestor worship. A reference to Nara survives in the dialogue, as a place the professor would have liked to take Noriko if there had been enough time.

Ozu's strategy, as Sorenson lays it out, is to invest each city with a significant set of moral associations. Tokyo is corrupt, Kyoto pure, Kamakura somewhere in between (it's only 30 miles from Tokyo, and the trains seem to be frequent, so it's presumably closer to corruption). Hattori makes his ambiguous concert suggestion in Tokyo, which is also where the Westernised divorcée Aya lives and works, while it is in Kyoto that Noriko renounces her selfishness and agrees to get married.

The trouble with such a schema is that to be convincing it needs to fit all the evidence. The professor works in Tokyo, for instance, but the city's corruption hasn't rubbed off on him. Sorenson makes much of the fact that it is in Tokyo that Noriko describes Onodera as 'filthy', as if it was the decadence of the place denouncing itself through her. He also tries to turn to advantage the fact that in Kyoto she expresses a different opinion about Onodera's decision to remarry. It doesn't really help, though, does it? It seems perverse to override the psychology of the film just so as to lay out an arbitrary geographical morality. After all we've been through, I'm not going to let *Late Spring* be turned into a sort of coded gazetteer of nostalgic militarism.

As for the presence of Kamakura in the screenplay, perhaps it has something to do with the fact that Ozu's co-writer Kogo Noda, newly reunited with him, had lived there since before the war. Ozu himself moved to Kamakura with his mother in April 1952. His grave is there. Possibly there was a logic of historical resonance underlying the choice, just as there may be people who move to Chelmsford for the thrill of living somewhere that was once, briefly, the capital city of England (from Monday, July the 1st to Saturday the 6th, 1381). But perhaps Ozu just thought Kamakura was a nice place to live.

As for Kyoto, yes, it's certainly a sort of Zen Disneyland. That's why it's still there. The Allies decided to spare it any bombing in the war – it's not as if the place had military significance, though destroying it would arguably have struck a blow against Japanese morale. Prayer is not heavy industry. It's easy for Kyoto to lay claim to an unworldly purity. That's what brings in the tourists, that's what pays the bills.

Sorenson's argument forces him into the position of saying that the SCAP censors were right all along, and that the subject of *Late Spring* is indeed arranged marriage. No social theme, after all, could better represent the old way of doing things.

It follows that Professor Somaya is a patriarch in the traditional mould, ministered to by his daughter: 'she will continuously be serving him tea, food, picking things up which he has dropped to the floor. Sometimes he gives short orders, not in an unfriendly manner, but as a matter of course and without any use of polite terms or sentence structures. He does not thank her, he does not ask her to please do this or that . . .'

It's at times like these that I wonder if I'm watching the same film as anyone else. The absence of 'please' and 'thank you' can betray a sense of entitlement, of exercised authority, yes, and it can also indicate a relationship so fluid that these formalities have long since fallen away.

And in the version of the film that I know, in the first scene in which Aya appears, after Noriko comes home and the two women go to her room, her father spontaneously brings tea and bread upstairs to them. It's at minute 39:11. And do they say, 'Why, professor, what's come over you? You're breaking with millennia of patriarchal precedent!'? No they do not. They wait until he's gone and then say, *Typical. He forgot the sugar. And the spoons!* It's hardly a special occasion.

Sorenson refers to the meal, but only to point out, in his discussion of the cultural associations of various foodstuffs, that the very words used to describe bread and jam, *pan to yam*, are borrowed from other languages, which would logically make it anti-traditional fare, and therefore suitable for Aya if no one else. Not a word about its being served by a supposedly traditional patriarch, who trots fondly upstairs with the supplies for the women's midnight feast. This is a low point in Sorenson's criticism.

It's also an effort for him to find anything particularly traditional about father's and daughter's behaviour in Kyoto, something his schema can't do without. He has to distort their exchanges wholesale to justify a reference to 'the final decision, taken by the father in Kyoto, that his only daughter must enter into an arranged marriage'. A travesty. It's true that the professor is more (hollowly) categorical about the need for the marriage here than anywhere else in the film, but his emotional state couldn't be further from the impersonal decision-making Sorenson suggests. He is clearly alarmed that Noriko, wanting to go on living with her father even after his remarriage, is opting for a sort of non-space, a disappearance, something not far short of social suicide. Her emotions are extreme at this point – it's her last appeal for clemency – and so are his. Bear in mind that any mention of actual suicide was automatically banned by the censors. This is a very dark moment psychologically, and the professor's banging the drum for marriage is thoroughly desperate, as well as thoroughly unpersuasive.

While the professor is packing his books, he holds one of them still for long enough for its title to be legible. It's *Also Sprach Zarathustra*, in English. Unlikely reading for a custodian of Confucian family values.

Underlying Sorenson's rhetorical efforts is an attack on a different 180° rule from the one normally mentioned in discussions of Ozu. That cinematic rule states, in the Wikipedia definition, 'that two characters (or other elements) in the same scene should always have the same left/right relationship to each other. If the camera passes over the imaginary axis connecting the two subjects, it is called crossing the line.' The 180° thesis as it applies to societies posits that drastic change, amounting to a U-turn, can be accomplished at short notice. This is the argument that Sorenson wants to take apart.

If an oil tanker heading for the rocks but still some miles off can't steer clear of disaster even with the wheel hard over, what is the likelihood of whole countries changing their ways to suit the priorities of those who have defeated them? Yet that is what is supposed to have happened in Japan at the end of the war.

Sorenson documents how soon after the Americans arrived in their country the image of the Japanese was reworked. From being denounced as fanatical sadists they were made over as good losers. An American journalist holed up in a hotel in Yokohama early in September 1945, more or less under house arrest while the military authorities assessed conditions on the ground, complained that 'correspondents belatedly receive handouts of translations from the Japanese press that are carefully edited and selected with a view to upholding the official Japanese line that "we were defeated but we hope the Americans will be as good as winners as we are as losers"'.

Sorenson's verdict on this is that 'there are no good losers, only good actors'. It's the best bit of phrasing in his book. He quotes from bewilderingly opposite descriptions of the national mood at the end of the war, with one authority (an article by John Dower) claiming that the military regime was falling apart of its own accord, while Akira Kurosawa in his autobiography makes out that only the Emperor's explicit counter-directive prevented a hundred million suicides.

Kurosawa's account appeared decades after the event, in 1982, and there's plenty of rhetoric in his memory of averted apocalyse. In any mass suicide, however well-run, there are always some ditherers, aren't there? The floating voters of voluntary death, the ones who have to be nudged quite brusquely towards the sword, the cliff-edge (as on the Japanese island of Saipan in 1944), the beaker of Kool-Aid. An act of concerted self-destruction is the wrong moment to get cold feet, but of course that's just the time it happens. The clean glory of the event slips away.

In his book Kurosawa describes the decision he took with some colleagues, in the event that the order for mass suicide was given (the Honourable Death of the Hundred Million), to take some of the military censors with him: 'We vowed to meet in front of the Ministry of the Interior and assassinate the censors before we took our own lives.' He seems to have had much more animosity towards them than towards the official enemy. The enemy might threaten his life, but the censors wanted to tamper with his work.

Despite Kurosawa's almost flagrant unreliability, Sorenson comes down more on that side of the scale. To him it seems obvious that a people saturated in nationalistic propaganda would be stubbornly attached to the priorities drummed into them for so long. And yet hasn't Japan behaved, in the half century or so since the war, less like the *Torrey Canyon* on its collision course for Pollard Rock and more like one of those trains with an engine at either end?

Hirohito even stayed where he was, in what had been the driver's seat, while corporate capitalism at the other end of the train decided the direction of travel and the speed. I imagine him blinking in confusion, still perched on the Chrysanthemum Throne but now facing a panel of disabled controls, and with his back to the direction of travel.

You could reasonably argue that the society resulting from the artificial yoking of elements facing in opposite directions has been reinforced, benefiting from some enviable internal bracing. An ingrained sense of responsibility to the larger group offers some immunity from the social dissolution likely to follow on from imposed economic freedoms.

Perhaps it's Sorenson's rather two-dimensional understanding of theatre that is the deficiency of his formulation about good actors and good losers (has he read Erving Goffman?). Even the best actors benefit from an effective script.

General de Gaulle, for instance, wrote a shrewd script for France after the Liberation, when he made out that collaboration was the choice of an anomalous minority of French people during the occupation. He made possible a theatricalised national unity whose run continued up to the time Marcel Ophuls made his documentary *The Sorrow and the Pity* in 1969, and even beyond. The negative corollary of this dramatic coherence was a slowness to find a place for things that didn't fit the script. It took a long time for France formally to take responsibility for the enthusiastic handing over of its Jews to the Germans. That didn't happen until February 2009.

At the end of his war, de Gaulle had the disadvantage of being a newly installed symbol of continuity, while the Japanese at the end of theirs could look to a familiar figurehead who was now saying unprecedented things in a recognisable style. What better could represent the apotheosis of *enryo*, those contortions of etiquette which save face by embracing humility, than the formula the emperor god found to describe defeat: 'the war has not necessarily developed in our favour'? It's the prototype of every humiliated football manager's post-match interview. *Frankly, this was not the result we were looking for . . .*

The indoctrinated population that Sorenson evokes would feel more abandoned, surely, by the sudden absence of instructions than by a familiar commander-in-chief telling them that he didn't want them to resist.

Sorenson thinks that the original audiences of a film like *Late Spring* read it against the grain, using the knowledge that everything they were permitted to see was censored by the forces of occupation. He points out that they were used to the idea of authorities intervening, as witness those time-lapse scenes of foreign kissing.

There's a difference, though, between a censorship that leaves obvious scars and one which is careful to clean up after itself. The stipulation made by the censorship agencies that film-makers must re-edit or re-shoot to mask any changes imposed on them wasn't simply a form of punishment. It recognised that smoothness of finish is a major part of the process by which a film colonises the imagination.

It may seem self-evident that knowledge of censorship will alter the experience of watching a film, but it isn't necessarily so. Art is built around absences anyway. Like consciousness, it is honeycombed with the things it doesn't know. The artificial removal of material need not violate the paradox of its integrity.

How many of us, for instance, watching classic Hollywood films, are surprised by the invariable separate beds of married couples? My bet is that most people make unconscious assumptions about American sleeping habits, rather than detecting the operation of the production code, originally set up to forestall formal censorship. And no doubt there were generations of young Americans who discovered with amazement, during adolescent explorations, that it was possible to take one foot off the floor while kissing, or even both of them, without calling down punitive lightning.

Perhaps too in post-war Japan there were audiences accustomed to the visual conjuring trick of the film kiss who were disappointed by the uncensored, unmagical version that was now permitted on the screen, perhaps even by kissing itself when they tried it.

Very occasionally a Hollywood film seems to refer to its own status as a product of censorship. The first scene of Gerd Oswald's *A Kiss Before Dying* (1956) is a tense discussion between two young people about the possibilities open to them in a difficult situation. It only makes sense if the audience reconstructs a sentence spoken there where the censor's scissors cannot reach, in the moment before the film began.

That was the non-existent moment when Joanne Woodward said to Robert Wagner, 'I'm pregnant.' The curious thing, though, is that to experience the film fully you need to forget its cunning evasion of the production code. It isn't easy to be inside and outside a film, while you're watching it. Cinema is a powerfully immersive medium. Films like *Out of the Past* or *2001* or *Black Narcissus* continue to make an impact even on television, shrunken in size and shot through with advertising jingles and alien flashing images, forced to defer to lesser technologies, to the doorbell, the kettle and the phone, humiliated in a domestic interior like kings sold into slavery. Being subliminally aware of censorship isn't at all the same thing as becoming a code-breaker. I hope I've shown that there are things about *Late Spring*, even on the level of plot, that haven't been noticed by experienced critics who have watched the film many more times than I have.

There are also plenty of things that others see that I don't. Kristin Thompson, for instance, categorically describes Somiya as an oldest son, though I can find no reference to his having brothers, either now or in the past. She also confidently describes Onodera as 'Professor'. As with Donald Richie so confidently referring to the death of Noriko's mother as recent, I don't say these statements are wrong, but I would love to know the evidence for them.

Onodera is comic relief incarnate, not far from an endearing buffoon (though he is also the catalyst for the film's theme of sexual distaste). His conversation with Somiya, as well as with Noriko, is largely teasing and childish. Somiya mentions the economist List, distinguishing the spelling of his name from the Hungarian composer's, and takes Nietzsche with him to read on holiday. Onodera (in the discussion about where the sea, the shrine and Tokyo are, from the professor's house) isn't convinced that the points of the compass are constant.

The evidence for his being a professor can only be the line of dialogue spoken by the barman at the Takigawa bar to Somiya and Aya when they're drinking *sake* there after Noriko's wedding: 'Professor Onodera came here with your daughter recently.' I wouldn't be in too much of a hurry to rely on that. This may be a courtesy title for any respectable customer (quite a middling level of bookishness, similarly, will get you addressed as *Professore* by the staff of an Italian restaurant), or perhaps the barman has seen him in Somiya's company and assumes that academics only socialise with their own kind.

All right, all right. I'm going to have to bluff this one out. It's true that when Onodera comes home with Noriko for *sake* (after the discussion of the filthiness involved in remarrying) Somiya asks him why he is visiting the area. 'Was it a business trip?' 'The Education Ministry again,' says Onodera.

So if I want to go on thinking that Onodera is a childhood friend of Somiya's who is now high up in a firm bidding for contracts to supply, say, roller towels to government institutions, then there's nothing much to stop me.

I suspect all I'm saying is that there's no actual correspondence between Onodera's supposed place in the world and the role he plays in the story. In a work of part-time realism, a character can be both an academic colleague (vice-chancellor, why not?) and a clueless buffoon.

If the blind spot in human eyesight was clearly labelled 'blind spot' then it wouldn't be one. It's the way the frayed patch of missing information seems to lead on, without a break, to the areas of functioning vision around it that makes it so treacherous.

The crucial distinction is not between continuity and discontinuity but between frank discontinuity and smoothed-over discontinuity. Since we structure the world to our satisfaction as much by suppressing aspects of it as by any other method, the continuity we detect and so much rely on is always likely to be the second sort of discontinuity, more or less expertly disguised. The internal censor never gets a day off. Nights are a different matter.

And even in dreams, the discontinuity only shows up after the event. At most there is a pocket of knowledge within the dream that this whole story doesn't add up, the equivalent in negative of the eye's blind spot, a seeing patch which doesn't have access to the whole picture and is as little joined up to the surrendering areas around it as its waking counterpart.

Sorenson expects a great deal of these audiences saturated with the propaganda of a previous regime: to see what is not there through the cracks of what is, piecing together a coherent set of attitudes for themselves, ignoring the conquerors' agenda foisted on the film-makers. If they can do that, then they haven't in fact been programmed by thousands of slogans, prescribing behaviour appropriate to a world that no longer exists. Instead they have learned to view films critically. In this respect they have been paradoxically Westernised, since it was one of the principles of CI&E to encourage 'individual initiative and enterprise' in tackling the problems of postwar Japan. Such sly deciphering of hidden messages is anything but passive and backward-looking.

Even though I'm not usually convinced by the way Sorenson marshals his material, there's no denying that he comes up with some startling new angles on the film.

The sequence of the train journey to Tokyo, for instance [at 10:51] with its odd, almost schoolboyish interest in the carriage ahead, as if the camera was yearning to inspect the locomotive, turns out to have some hidden meanings. As Sorenson explains it, the point of several shots is to make sure that audiences get a glimpse of the white stripe running along the side of that carriage.

A little later there's a shot of the train from the side, to underline the point. The white line is clearly visible. Ozu has a more than casual interest in its being noticed, since the stripe meant something very specific to the film's original audience. It meant 're-served for occupation personnel only'.

It's the sort of illuminating moment that vindicates Sorenson's whole enterprise, and it doesn't take long for him to push his advantage, by making out that the carriage of the forces of occupation, unseen and not to be shown, shapes the whole sequence. That's why the carriage is so crowded. Japanese nationals were forbidden from entering such places, so the rest of the train is correspondingly full. That's why there's no seat available for either father or daughter at the beginning of their journey, before the thinning out of numbers which makes available first one seat (taken by him) and then two.

I can't help feeling that this gives too much explanatory power to the new discovery. The shots of the train from outside make it clear that there is only the one striped carriage on the whole of the train. One reserved carriage out of nine, even if sparsely occupied (though that's pure guesswork, since we aren't in a position to count heads), will have some effect on the crowding of the train, but isn't enough by itself to make the difference between passenger comfort and being jammed together like battery hens or, indeed, present-day commuters without forces of occupation to blame for their discomfort.

The way that seats become available in the course of the journey doesn't really add up in naturalistic terms either. Both Noriko and her father are going to central Tokyo, she to a hospital, then on to a shopping trip, he to his work at the University. We don't see them leaving the train, though the implication of the dialogue is that his stop is before hers. If institutions, both medical and academic, and shopping streets are all centrally located then it seems surprising that the carriage should empty out as it approaches that area. I'm not claiming any actual knowledge of the layout of Tokyo, but barring revelations about city geography it seems likely that the train sequence, despite its very pointed reference to contemporary

renson doesn't discuss the oddity of this, a
t breach of regulations that had no conse-
s. One possibility is that the agencies' opera-
njoyed the joke at their expense, and saw no
in squashing something that wouldn't mean
uch outside that room (a room in the same
g as the one on the screen) – yet the chuckle
ulgence is hardly a keynote in dealings be-
he censors and the censored.

esn't it seem more likely that in the summer
9 responsibility was being partially shifted
n American bureaucracy to a Japanese one,
zu profited from a relaxation in scrutiny?
s at this point in the evolution of the system,
d films were rubber-stamped rather than fully
ed.

here were objections after all, Ozu wasn't
much of a risk with the substituted establish-
ts. He was dipping only a toe in the waters
nce. In the event of CI&E cutting up rough
nanding a re-edit, he need only have stock
of Tokyo ready. The shot of the Coca-Cola
he sequence of Noriko and Hattori's trip to
ch is similarly not in the script, but again,
ould have been no special difficulty involved
ving it.

more ambitious show of mischief would
volved a greater risk. If for instance Ozu
ck to the original script, and filmed the odd

conditions of travel, is primarily concerned with portraying the father-daughter relationship and the subtle way it is modified in a public setting, at the expense of some strict plausibility in the modelling of post-war public transport outcomes.

It's at the end of the train sequence that Sorenson scores a real bullseye, even two of them in a row. Kristin Thompson is a fine and nuanced critic, who spotted for instance Noriko's discordant handbag in the opening scene, and it's not her fault that in the train sequence she detects only some moments of 'amusing byplay with eyelines'. And this is how she describes the film's arrival in Tokyo, in her book *Breaking the Glass Armor*:

Sometimes Ozu uses more shots than would be needed to establish a locale; in *Late Spring*, for example, he shows a view of the Hattori building at the beginning of a sequence in which Noriko is shopping and meets an old friend, Professor Onodera. The initial shot serves to indicate that the area is the Ginza, since the Hattori building is perhaps the most famous of that district. But then Ozu shows another view of that same building, which yields no new information.

Well, it depends on what you mean by information. In the approved script, Tokyo was supposed to be 'established' by a bird's-eye view of the city, an entirely conventional shot. In 1949, though, the Hattori building meant something more specific than just 'Tokyo' or 'the Ginza'. It meant the PX (it stands for Post Exchange), the place where occupation forces went to buy supplies.

The PX was like a huge white-striped no-Japanese-allowed railway carriage bursting with condoms, cigarettes and chewing gum, and the streets around it would have been seething with horny, nicotine-addicted GIs, bearing down on defenceless sticks of Juicy Fruit with their strong imperialistic jaws. The PX would also have been a magnet for black-marketeers, though their activities were banned from appearing in any occupation-approved film.

The disparity between the real Hattori building and its simulacrum in *Late Spring*, serene and deserted (perhaps filmed in the early morning), is a joke that any Tokyo resident in the film's first audiences would immediately have understood.

But why two shots of the same building? Perhaps because the building itself had more than one purpose, one identity. The PX was based on the ground floor, but on a higher level the building contained the offices of the censorship agencies. This was the site of their various conferences and discussions. So when Ozu used the Hattori building as a way of establishing Tokyo he was also showing audiences the place he was required to come for permission to proceed, first with his synopsis and then with his script, every time he wanted to make a film.

So the anomalous double presentation of a clichéd

Tokyo landmark is almost
formation, though not in r
whole point – any verbal re
itself automatically censore
late stage of production to
proto-postmodernist joke.
sorship could be reinserte
governed by otherwise in
that were themselves taboc
couldn't say what he wan
show the building where t

If the building's fun(
PX would be familiar to
*Spring*'s first audiences, it
less widely known. Inside
narrower one, only a tin
private joke.

On the other hand, t
who would infallibly get t
agency functionaries wh
the film before granting
their being slow on the u
chance of showing the E
movies of the Forbidden
your camerawork. No (
would be nodding off
the ticklish question of 1
chosen, about which th
had even been broachec

S
flagra
quenc
tives
virtue
very 1
buildi
of inc
tween
D
of 19
from
and C
Perha
finishe
inspec
If
taking
ing sh
of defi
and d
footag
sign in
the be
there v
in rem
An
have i
had stu

stand-off between father and daughter after the Noh play in a tableau of war damage, at the very least he would need to have more innocuous footage to hand – and the antagonism he had revealed might have led to greater penalties than the neutral directive to re-edit. The same goes for the baseball game he shows [at 42:00], before Noriko's big scene with Masa, which was originally supposed to take place in a burnt-out building. The occupation authorities encouraged baseball, both as a sport and as an element in films, on the basis that it promoted the everyday democracy of teamwork. Filming a game in charred ruins would be uncomfortably close to a black joke.

I can muster some sort of corroboration for the rubber-stamping idea, using material from Sorenson's book (though these are not his interpretations). There was another film passing through the system in the late spring and summer of 1949, Kurosawa's *Stray Dog*, and here too a blind eye was turned to a certain amount of non-compliance, with officially discouraged script elements surviving into the finished film.

The synopsis discussion for *Stray Dog* took place two months after the one for *Late Spring*, on 14 June, just after authority for censorship had been transferred to the Film Ethics Regulation Control Committee (usually known as EIRIN). The single element of Kurosawa's script that caused most concern to EIRIN was, oddly, the use of a real hotel name, the Metro. It was felt that this might infringe the civil rights of the staff – itself a strange, rather parochial priority for the forces of occupation, concentrating on the sensibilities of a handful of Japanese workers rather than the great project of reshaping their country around them. Kurosawa duly changed the name of the hotel.

The censors also stipulated that the use of army uniform be avoided. This he ignored. The most famous sequence in the film is a nine-minute montage of Toshiro Mifune walking the hot and squalid city streets, wearing uniform. Impossible for Kurosawa to have filmed innocuous shots at the same time, for safe re-editing – and, again, the blatant disobedience of what he was doing would make any safety-net of footage pointless. Yet there the montage is, forbidden yet allowed to stand.

Granted, Kurosawa had a confrontational, risk-taking side of his character, unlike Ozu, but he also knew at first hand (from the farrago of *Desertion at Dawn*) how obstructive the authorities could be. For both stroppy Kurosawa and slyly impervious Ozu to get away with infractions in summer 1949 suggests that they knew what they were doing, as if some covert softening of the system was known to them both, making it safe to call the bluff of censorship, in small matters.

There are elements of defiance in both *Stray*

*Dog* and *Late Spring*, despite their almost caricatural contrast with each other, but it needs to be said that they don't rise above the tokenistic. They're no more than trace-elements. Kurosawa may have been acting out the arch-adolescent statement 'You don't tell me what to do!', but actually they did, and they went on doing so until the end of the occupation. The censors disapproved of films showing signage in English, and Sorenson makes rather a meal of the presence in *Stray Dog* of two shots where Toshiro Mifune stands by a wall on which the words 'Loading Bay for Special Service' can be read. Would that really have had a strong effect on contemporary audiences of the film? It hardly seems inflammatory, and Ozu, too, showed English-language signage in *Late Spring* without riot, reprimand or repercussion.

The real impact of *Stray Dog*, surely, was its *film noir* atmosphere of simmering disillusion, itself an import from foreign cinema. If Kurosawa was fighting Westernisation, he was using Westernised weapons to do it. He may have seemed to come from nowhere at the time of *Rashomon*'s breakthrough in the West, but this was to some extent a re-absorption by the West of an exoticised version of its own approach to cinema. No critic in Japan ever worried that the West didn't understand Kurosawa.

The enduring opposition between Ozu and Kurosawa, seeming neutrality and heroic confrontation, has parallels in other art forms (Mozart and

Beethoven, Vermeer and Rembrandt), and as always tends to obscure any common ground. Such pairings have an inbuilt tendency to favour the more embattled of the two. Ozu didn't live some sort of hermetic Japanese existence, and any apparent alignment with the past on his part shouldn't be allowed to blot out his vivid interest in the present. If he wasn't drawn to contemporary darkness, and controversial subjects (crime, disease, prostitution, black marketeeering) as Kurosawa was, still he wasn't exactly hiding from the changes in his world.

Sorenson's assumption, for instance, that Aya is essentially a cautionary figure (this is what happens to young women who follow their hearts) doesn't do justice to the charm of the portrait. Aya isn't indulged, but she's more than a foil for the other characters, and her outlook on life isn't patronised or squelched.

Perhaps it was just that, a portrait. At first the censorship procedure required synopses and scripts to be submitted only in Japanese, for translation in-house. Then the system was changed, with material to be submitted in both the relevant languages.

Doesn't that mean that Ozu had fairly extensive dealings with translators into English, and typists who could handle the language? Sorenson describes SCAP as 'permanently in want of typists and stenographers with English-language skills', as is borne out by the ads in contemporary newspapers. The same description must apply to Japanese film studios, which had to prepare English versions of synopses and scripts for the benefit of the censors.

It doesn't seem all that silly to suggest that models for Aya, stenographer able to cope with English and oddly sympathetic breaker of marriage vows, might have been found in these ranks. The alternative is to posit the film's portrait as pure abstracted moralising, with no taint of observation or lived experience. But it hardly seems a sermon in celluloid.

The documentation of *Late Spring*'s passing through the censorship process is unusually full. The script submitted for approval, for instance, included a scene in which Noriko runs into a family friend who invites her to a baseball game. This family friend doesn't appear anywhere else in the script, which leads Sorenson to speculate that this scene was written as a sort of sop, a bargaining chip, since the censorship authorities were so famously fond of the game. By this interpretation Ozu never intended to film it, but put it into the script as a piece of propaganda, a way of establishing his adherence to the agenda of the occupiers, in the hope that they would overlook any falling short, elsewhere in his film, from the approved tones and subjects.

It's possible. But if there's the slightest justification for the unwieldy and jostling bureaucracy set up by SCAP, it's that having separate agencies charged with removing negative material and promoting the positive made this sort of horse-trading impossible. CI&E might be tickled to death by your many captivating baseball scenes, but that wouldn't stop CCD from coming down hard on you if you were foolish enough to refer to corruption or censorship.

In any case, Ozu's use of baseball as a theme isn't entirely controlled by irony. Aya, for instance, explicitly invokes an innings of baseball as the model for a modern woman's romantic life. Her failed marriage was Strike One, but she'll get it right next time. This is all potentially satirical: if arranged marriage is a hallowed social structure with a ritual significance, then modern marriage is no more than a game.

Oh dear, I hope these baseball details are accurately translated in the subtitles.

The next shot is of a baseball game in progress, and what does it show? The batter missing the first ball pitched to him, then connecting strongly with the second, that's what. Ozu was free to show any pattern of play, or none at all. In the few seconds he chooses to include, he settles on exactly the scenario of Aya's hopeful fantasy. That's not how a film-maker goes about undercutting a character's illusions.

The baseball theme carries over into the next scene, of Noriko talking to her nephew Bu-chan, not yet aware that she's been invited to Masa's house to discuss the marriage she doesn't want. Bu-chan is dressed to play baseball but is crying at being excluded from the game – perhaps the game we just saw is the one he's missing, though the uncertainty principle expressed by Ozu's whole approach to his art makes me hesitate to state it as a fact.

There's nothing sinister about Bu-chan's exclusion, it's just that the 'enamel' on his baseball bat (enamel or simply paint?) isn't yet dry. His painting has also marked Masa's interior, and he's in disgrace as a result.

Naturally enough, Bu-chan is dressed to play baseball, while his mother is in traditional costume, as always. She can't impose a dress code on the next generation, which seems to take to Westernised pastimes and gratifications without any prompting. But there's a bit more to it than that.

Masa herself is not altogether hostile to Western influences. She's the one who recommended young Mr Satake as having a (partial) facial resemblance to Gary Cooper, specifically as he appeared in a baseball film – it must be *Pride of the Yankees*, from 1942. So even Masa the traditionalist has been marginally indoctrinated.

In one of the strangest interventions in the script of *Late Spring*, the censors objected to the specifying of Gary Cooper in the reference to Satake's appearance. They thought there should be a more general invocation of good looks, but Ozu stayed defiantly loyal to his original formula. From this distance it seems absurd to seek to instil Western democratic

225

values into a defeated enemy, only to declare Gary Cooper off limits as an object of desire.

The camera stays on Masa's son Bu-chan in his room, still wearing his baseball uniform, after he has been told that he has been grounded on account of the enamel incident. He mimes some fierce baseball pitching [43:27], aiming the invisible ball at the door which his mother has just closed. It's very obvious that she, rather than the door, is the target. Just as furniture makes possible, or inhibits, certain transactions between people, so costume offers licence or imposes restraint. Bu-chan would never act out these aggressive gestures if he was wearing traditional costume, but the baseball uniform amplifies his resentment. This would all be very disturbing if Aunt Masa didn't have things altogether too much her own way for so much of the film, with the result that any kind of resistance seems healthy and desirable.

Lars-Martin Sorenson brings two things to the study of *Late Spring*, a mass of evidence and an interpretation. Unfortunately the interpretation stubs its toes on the evidence. The themes he singles out, such as characterisation by food and drink and ingratiation by baseball, don't bear out his idea of Ozu as a traditionalist sending coded messages of symbolic historical resistance. All Ozu's characters, including Aunt Masa, are dealing in different ways with a new world, to which nostalgia isn't a possible response. And perhaps Ozu's angle on the past, the recent rather than the distant past, is not as indulgent as Sorenson makes out.

There's a strange moment early on in the film, during the conversation between Onodera and Noriko's father, while she's warming the *sake* for them. The dialogue leads on from the discussion of her health, and the fact that the result of some test or other has gone down to 15, which is a good sign (we're given no clue about what unit is being measured by this number). It goes like this:

Onodera: 'She looks fine. It was all because of forced labour in the war.'

Somiya: 'And she had to run around to get some food on her day off.'

Onodera: 'What a bad time. No wonder she suffered.'

They chuckle.

It's the only reference in the whole film to anything that happened in the war. The only other mentions of hostilities are more in the nature of chronological markers, as when the professor talks about making his first visit to Kyoto since the war, or Masa describes Satake's father as the director of Nitto Chemicals before the war.

The sketch of Noriko's war is presented rather as Chekhov manages things in his plays, where the opening situation of the drama is expounded in Scene One. Two people rehearse information they both already have, presumably for our benefit. But why do we need to know these facts? They're never referred to again.

Like so many of Ozu's choices, this moment is both puzzling and highly deliberate. In a screenplay loosely based on a pre-war novel, there can be no question of it being part of the source material. It has been included for a reason. But why should Noriko in particular be felt to have suffered in the war? Her contemporary and schoolmate Aya doesn't seem to have experienced anything comparable.

'Forced labour' is a strong phrase, usually associated with prisons. The hard labour to which Oscar Wilde was sentenced broke his health. Someone made to carry out forced labour would not normally live at home, and would therefore lack the protection of family. The mention of 'days off' doesn't quite fit this picture. The phrases 'forced labour' and 'days off' belong in different worlds.

The first time I saw *Late Spring* I was very struck by this scrap of dialogue. Blame those few unemphatic lines for this whole book. From that moment on, I was on a quest. I was on a mission. Actually I just went to the library, but it comes to the same thing.

The censors who saw the script of *Late Spring* were also struck by this exchange, and drew attention to an 'unnecessary' mention of the war. It's hard to disagree, except that Ozu clearly felt it was necessary in some way. The original script specified that Noriko's forced labour was 'in the Navy'. Ozu left things vague in the final film – but he resisted the pressure to cut the mention of the war, and forced labour, altogether. He even added a line to the scene, the one about 'days off', though Sorenson supplies a slightly different translation, saying that Noriko 'spent her rare holidays scrounging for food'.

So this little bit of conversation between Onodera and the professor has deeper roots in the process of making the film than the famous vase, that Johnny-come-lately of timeless meaning, which isn't in the script. Not only was this piece of dialogue there from the beginning, but Ozu defied the censorship authorities to keep it, after they objected. His motive wasn't sly humour, as it was in the case of the Hattori building (though at least half of that twinned joke would have been lost on the original audience). His motive must have been something serious.

So what am I saying? Well, that what we have is a wisp of back story according to which the heroine has been ill-treated in some way, while the whole story is concerned with her reluctance to get married. If the point is to explain why her marriage prospects haven't been considered before, then bad health not related to the war would make for a cleaner plot point.

Japanese films are so shrouded in a protective

critical atmosphere of exoticism that audiences don't think to make a connection between the whispered damage and the strange reluctance. That would break the lovely oriental spell. Film-goers don't have any difficulty with the idea that, say, *My Beautiful Laundrette* is 'about' Thatcherism, but would never dare to wonder if *Late Spring* doesn't refer in some way to sexual trauma. Cultures that put certain styles of femininity on a pedestal can be very punitive to the unprotected and unrespectable.

Isn't it as if an academic industry had grown up around Henry James's magnificent suggestiveness, his occluded precision, with no one quite liking to mention the passage where the governess remembers the strange day when Maisie came home in tears without her unmentionables? (Please note: I know of no such passage. This for analogical purposes only. One bombshell per essay quite enough.)

The test of a worthwhile interpretation is that it should enrich the work of art rather than impoverish it. If Noriko was raped or sexually abused in the course of her forced wartime labour, away from the protection of her father and her class status, then it certainly explains her deep aversion to the sexual venture of marriage. Every other element in the film remains in place, though her susceptibility to Hattori gains in poignancy. Only feeble interpretations, of which there are plenty, need to move over or look around nervously for the exit.

230

The tragedy which so many viewers have felt from the ending gains intensity from the vinegar-splash of irony. In his concern for a fulfilment which may not even be a possibility, Noriko's father edges her out of the position that has provided her with security and happiness. No wonder she clings so desperately to the role of dutiful daughter, that precious position which can allow a woman to stand aside from the marriage market without loss of status. Fatherly love drives her from the refuge fatherly love has offered. The rescuer throws her from the lifeboat.

Sorenson's book concerns itself with overtones of resistance to the occupation regime, but it must be obvious that a reference to wartime forced labour says nothing discreditable about the new administration. Censors objected to this part of the script on the general grounds of its being backward-looking, when official policy was that bygones should be bygones, and not because there was any criticism of America involved.

Raking up the past would hardly be popular with the domestic audience either. Picking at old scabs on the body politic isn't an activity that makes friends. If Ozu really was trying to address the issue of the sexual abuse of women in wartime, then he couldn't risk anything above the level of the hint, not only because the censors would pounce but because his fellow-countrymen would resent any reminder of the degradations of conflict. The intimation of Noriko's suffering is like so many of the themes in the film. It doesn't build to a resolution, but it doesn't go away.

What was Ozu's own experience of war? He made nationalistic films promoting the military endeavour and also, disconcertingly, served as a censor himself – making him one of the people whom Kurosawa had vowed to kill before committing suicide, in the event that the Emperor gave the order for self-destruction. The director of *Living* might have annihilated the director of *Good Morning* before either film was made.

Kurosawa's melodramatic claims to a willingness to kill himself and others sound very strained, but there is a little family history to back it up indirectly. The *benshi* was a conservative force in the Japanese film system, whose popularity delayed the arrival of sound (Ozu continued to make silent films, after all, right up to *The Only Son* in1936).

The first talkie to cause a sensation was Josef von Sternberg's *Morocco* in 1930, and quite right too. No one should be expected to resist Dietrich kissing a legionnaire's wife as part of her nightclub act. The first all-talking Japanese film followed the next year. But the *benshi* weren't finished.

In 1932 the *benshi* of Nikkatsu studios went on strike against a policy which put cinemas showing foreign films under pressure to fire their *benshi*.

The strike failed, and its leader committed suicide as a result. This was Heigo Kurosawa, Akira's older brother and a celebrated *benshi* in his own right.

If this historical episode hasn't found its way into a film, I really can't see why. It has everything, particularly if the narrator is a veteran *benshi* brought out of retirement to explain the intricacies of *Rashomon* and having a flashback to the good old, bad old days.

The earlier of the two regimes of censorship being discussed here, the one so deeply resented by Akira Kurosawa, is unlikely to have had any leeway in it, of the sort that lent the American-run system its mysterious moments of yielding.

Ozu made two films during the war (*Brothers and Sisters of the Toda Family*, 1941, *There Was a Father*, 1942) and perhaps they'll take their place in the BFI's Ozu retrospective on DVD, begun in 2010. These were nationalistic films promoting the military endeavour rather than outright propaganda, and Ozu the acclaimed humanist seems, in at least one unmade script commissioned in 1942 (intended to glorify the Burma campaign), to have had an unexpectedly hard-edged attitude to things such as maiming, sickness and death, which propaganda normally leaves in soft focus. (I have to go by Sorenson's descriptions.) The title – *The Land of our Parents so Far Away* – is rather more dreamy than the script he submitted. The censors were

confronted with almost caustic bits of realism, such
as a 'thousand-stitch belt' (*senninbari*), one of the
many that were communally made by civilians and
given to servicemen to raise morale, being described
as crawling with 'goddesses of mercy', apparently a
military euphemism for 'lice'. Ozu was sometimes
scornful of the sanitised, reverential tone of other
directors' war films.

The tone of this unmade script seems closer in
American terms to Samuel Fuller than John Ford.
The two films which were actually made lay stress
on self-sacrifice as a virtues in families as much as in
servicemen. The tone of *The Land of our Parents so
Far Away* is very different, coarse and almost nihilis-
tic in its militarism, to judge by the song sung at one
point, to a traditional tune:

> We take a piss from the Great Wall of China
> And make a rainbow over the Gobi.
> As the fog clears in London
> See the *koinobori* [traditional carp banners] fluttering
>     high!
> In the streets of Chicago thick with gangsters
> Raise a memorial stone for our grandchildren to
>     remember us by . . .

Nothing about the glory of the Emperor or the justice
of the cause, just global rampage and death-wish.

It's possible to fantasise a narrative in which
Ozu deliberately sabotaged the propaganda film he

was commissioned to make by taking an objection-able tone – as an ex-censor himself he could hardly claim ignorance of the rules – and was consequently punished by being drafted in June 1943 (he had already seen action). This seems rather overdramatic, in fact positively Hollywood, but in the absence of evidence about why the film wasn't made it isn't fair to assume that Ozu was fully committed to the imperialistic project either.

Still, if I'm saying that censorship enriched Ozu's procedures when he came to make *Late Spring*, I have to acknowledge the force of the same proposition as applied to the earlier set of restrictions. Noel Burch goes further, suggesting in his 1979 book *To the Distant Observer* that the two wartime films, *Brothers and Sisters of the Toda Family* and *There Was a Father*, represent 'the plateau/peak of Ozu's mature development'. His argument is that Western film conventions never really dovetailed with traditional Japanese aesthetics, so that the closing of cultural borders associated with the rise of militarism had the fringe benefit of allowing Japanese film-makers to refine their own style. By this reckoning the cultural atmosphere of Japanese fascism, unlike its European counterparts, wasn't necessarily retrogressive in artistic terms.

This is a point of view that takes some absorbing, pulling apart as it does the tidy join we're used to making between oppressive regimes and artistic decadence. It administers a salutary shock. (Leni Riefenstahl remained such a controversial figure because of the nagging suspicion that her artistic procedures couldn't simply be dismissed as decadent, ideologically tainted.) It's a tonic with a bitter taste, intellectual Fernet Branca to chase the hangover of lazy assumptions. It would also take a lot of specialist knowledge to engage with, let alone contradict.

As for Ozu's post-war work, to Burch it represents 'the history of a gradual fossilisation', a 'petrification in academic rigidity'. This, in fact, is when decadence sets in. The films after 1942 display a 'frozen academicism'. He lumps together Ozu's output in this period of decline, making a partial exception for *Record of a Tenement Gentleman*. To me, *Late Spring* is fresh rather than stale, fluid rather than stiff, vibrant with incompatible meanings, very far from being set in the stone of self-parody or self-pastiche. As seen from the particular angle of *To the Distant Observer*, this quiet, small film from 1949 isn't even distinctive enough to merit individual dismissal. Though there are over four hundred films in Burch's index, this isn't one of them.

If there were shameful things on the home front that Ozu had witnessed or heard about, then obviously he couldn't refer to them in a film made while the war was going on – and he couldn't do so afterwards either. The period between the collapse of military censorship and the establishment of SCAP's authority wasn't long. It lasted six weeks. In this interregnum with no censorship there was nothing else either: no light bulbs, no reliable supply of electricity. Film stock was substandard and the cameras knackered. There weren't even any nails to hold scenery together. Any rough approximation to a shooting schedule would inevitably be disrupted when cast and crew ran short of food and had to go foraging for it. Not a golden moment to make films of any sort.

I don't even mind if my suggestion about Noriko's sexual trauma falls flat. Perhaps like the Reverend Timothy Fortune in Sylvia Townsend Warner's novel I will make a single convert after years of preaching, and lose my faith on the same day. I can't reasonably pretend this is what *Late Spring* is 'really about', after everything I've tried to suggest about the misdirected, the discontinuous, the indeterminate. I do mind, though, if it's just ruled out of court. The otherworldly calm of Japanese cinema in the post-war years is something we cling to as an idea, when the single most obvious thing about these films is that everyone involved in them was traumatised by war, privation and defeat. If we choose to take the Noriko smile at face value, it's because we choose to think that the Japanese didn't actually mind being fire-bombed and irradiated, that they kept the old Zen calm going when they saw the Sumida river, weeks after an air raid on

Tokyo, choked with charred and bloated corpses. We have a strong vested interest in their serenity.

Statement of the obvious, the obvious that no one ever seems to get round to mentioning: there is more than one sort of war damage, and more than one way of portraying it.

Ozu is routinely enshrined as a timeless master of transcendent subtlety, as if you could be subtle in the abstract without having a subject to be subtle about ('life' doesn't count!). We accept the idea of his sublime indirectness, as long as he's not saying anything. There couldn't be a more patronising way of acknowledging greatness.

If we like to see his films as being about everything in general, nothing in particular, then that expresses a preference, and it's not difficult to work out why we value this interpretation so highly. We're grateful for some Zen vagueness. We don't really want to know what's behind Noriko's smile.

In the process we happily go along with the obvious untruth that great art is immortal. Of course art is mortal, just as mortal as the people who make it, but in a different way. In the long run it's the museum curator, defending treasures from handling, who is the real vandal. Works of art have more to fear from the embalming process than from straightforward rust or rot.

The question of whether sexual trauma is part of the intended subject matter of *Late Spring* isn't something that can be settled as a matter of fact. It's a speculation that may or may not be the case – though academic's-daughter-mysteriously-damaged-by-forced-labour isn't something you'd make up on a whim at a script conference, particularly if no one else in the film you were making has any wartime experiences attached to them. So try looking at the logic of it from the other angle. Reverse the argument. If Yasujiro Ozu did decide to make a film about a sexually traumatised woman and the effects of her experiences on her family life in post-war Japan, within the limits of what the censors and his audience could accept, what would it look like? Wouldn't it look like *Late Spring*? Very much like *Late Spring*.

nh   Notting Hill Editions

Notting Hill Editions is devoted to the best in essay writing. Our authors, living and dead, cover a broad range of non-fiction, but all display the virtues of brevity, soul and wit.

Our books are only part of our offering. Our commitment to reinvigorating the essay as a literary form extends to our website, where our Essay Journal is regularly updated with newly commissioned short essays as well as news and opinions on essay writing. The website also hosts a wonderful Essay Library, a home for the world's most important and enjoyable essays, including the facility to search, save your favourites and add your comments and suggestions.

To discover more, please visit
www.nottinghilleditions.com